Enjoy Your Bible

IRVING L. JENSEN

moody press
chicago

Printed in the United States of America

Contents

"Did not our hearts

GLOW WITHIN US

 while He

was talking to us on the road and

OPENED THE SCRIPTURES to us?"

(Luke 24:32 Berkeley Version)

Introduction

READING AND STUDYING the Bible is a basic requirement for the Christian's growth, and happily it can be one of his most enjoyable experiences from day to day.

Why do not more Christians enjoy the Bible as fully as they may? Perhaps because many have not tasted the joys of first-hand discoveries of the Bible's priceless gems. They absorb much of what is spoken or written by others, but they are not motivated to move on from there to search the Scriptures on their own.

Confucius, the Chinese teacher of ancient days, said, "I give a pupil one corner of a subject, and if he cannot find the other three corners, I do not want him to be my pupil." Let us apply this to Bible study, and pose a practical question. *What will motivate a student to study on his own?* Whatever this motivation is, it is clear that it will involve the three God-given facilities which every person has: intellect, emotions and will. Bible study can be truly enjoyable when it challenges the intellect, stirs the emotions, and directs the will.

The author once heard this remark by a student of a Bible class concerning first-hand study: "This makes Bible study fun!" Someone might wish the student had used a more sophisticated word than "fun" to apply to Bible study, but second thoughts might bring other conclusions. For, you see, this student had begun to experience, in his God-given emotional makeup, the exciting joy of discovering truths in the Bible which

5

he had never seen before. Things were stirring up inside of him, a happy environment for the activities of his intellect and will. He was beginning to actually ENJOY the Bible.

Let us make a personal application. Answer honestly this question, "What would spur you on to do more Bible study on your own?" However you might word your reply, the likely answer would be, "The enjoyment of it." We were created with something inside that is attracted to enjoyment and satisfaction. The world finds its expression in the pleasures of sin, temporary though they be. Can good and pure activities, like Bible study, be pleasurable, *truly* pleasurable? The answer is yes. Believers of all ages since the Bible was written have testified to such satisfaction. The psalmist called his emotion-packed experience with God's Word *"delightful"* (Ps. 119:24). The very Lord who caused the hearts of the two disciples to burn within them as He opened the Scriptures to them (Luke 24:32) can give the same exhilarating experience to Christians today. Bible study *can* be stimulating, interesting, delightful, comforting, sobering, calming, challenging. In being this, it is truly enjoyable.

The chapters of this book, containing methods as well as illustrations and exhortations, have been written to help transport the reader from the doldrums of an unexciting relationship to the Bible to the joys and thrills of a personal and growing involvement. As you read each chapter, remember that you—whoever you are—can fully ENJOY your Bible.

APPRECIATING THE BIBLE

Chapter 1

Appreciating What the Bible Is

MILLIONS OF PEOPLE TODAY own a copy of the Scriptures. It would be interesting to know what proportion of these fully appreciate what a precious gem the Bible is. Appreciation of the Bible is a first step to enjoying it.

What really is the Bible, anyway? Where did it come from? Who wrote it? How did it get here? What does it say? What makes it such a unique book?

Let us look for some answers to these questions. If we as Christians need to spend much time with the Bible, we surely should know what the Bible really is.

I. THE BIBLE IS A MIRACLE BOOK.

We all know that the Bible is a book of miracles, in that it *records* miracles. But are we aware that the very existence of the Bible is a miracle in itself? Let us look at this more closely.

A. The Bible is a miracle as to its *birth*.

W. E. Gladstone once said, "The Bible is stamped with a Specialty of Origin, and an immeasurable distance separates it from all competitors." The Bible is a unique book. Just as no one can describe the miracle of life in the birth of a baby, so no one can describe the miraculous birth of God's Book, the Bible. God says the Book came into being by His breath (II Tim. 3:16). That is how His universe also was created (Ps. 33:6), and who can explain *that* miracle? God further says that the human authors of the Scriptures "spoke from God" as they were "borne along by the Holy Spirit" (II Peter 1:21, literal translation). Though they had the free exercise of their native abilities, emotions, thoughts, and vocabularies, whatever they wrote was infallible and in perfect accord with the divine will, for they were "borne along by the Holy Spirit." The human writers themselves were fallible, but their work in writing was infallible, because of this divine control. No other book was written in this particular manner. Its birth was truly a miracle.

B. The Bible is a miracle as to its sixty-six individual books gradually *growing* into one unit, called the canon.

These books, written by about forty authors over a period of some fifteen hundred years, are more than just a collection of diverse writings. In ways known only to God, and under His superintendence, the canon came into being. All the writings—no more and no less—which God uniquely inspired for His Book are now bound in the *one* volume. And that volume has *one* major theme: the salvation of God offered to sinful man by Jesus Christ. The Holy Bible—one book made up of 66 books—could not be, without the miracle.

C. The Bible is also a miracle as to its *transmission* through the thousands of scribal copyings into the modern printing era.

The ancient scribes making copies of the books of the Bible occasionally committed errors of eye, ear and memory, for their work, unlike that of the original authors, was not divinely intended to be infallible. But God supernaturally kept any one error from growing in the course of the centuries to the proportion where it might have contaminated the corpus of manuscripts of any generation, and so jeopardized a vital teaching of the Scriptures. The purity of the Bible text is even better than that suggested by the famous soap slogan, "99 44/100% pure." No other writing, exposed to similar processes of propagation, can match such accuracy of transmission. Only God's master control over the scribal processes can account for this.

D. The Bible is a miracle as to its very *survival* through all the centuries.

Apathy and disuse, worm and rot, and even the command of a Roman emperor, Diocletian, in A.D. 303, that all the Scriptures be destroyed by fire, have not removed them from the scene. Today millions revere the Bible as God's Holy Book despite the subtle attempts of liberal theologians to humanize it as a mere product of man. It has survived the hammer blows of the skeptics of the ages. The inscription on the monument to the Huguenots of Paris expresses this so vividly: "Hammer away, ye hostile hands; your hammers break; God's anvil stands."

E. The Bible is a miracle as to its world-wide reception and influence.

It is the most published book in the world because the world continues to seek its counsel and revelation of the truth. As an example of the Bible's public acceptance, six million copies of *Today's English Version* were in circulation within a year of its publication, despite the fact that there had been no special promotion in advance of its appearance.

Of all the books ever written, the Bible is the only

9

one that fully understands man. Its phenomenal impact on the souls of men, the hearths of homes and the halls of nations can be recognized, but never fully measured. This is because it is more than a book—it is the very life-giving breath of God.

TRULY THE BIBLE IS A MIRACLE BOOK! And from a practical standpoint the most wonderful thing about this is that God *gave this miracle book to us* for our own personal benefit, to show us where we came from, where we are going, and how to live in the meantime. The book might be called a *manual* for living. Let us look at this further.

II. THE BIBLE IS A MANUAL FOR LIVING.

Have you ever thought of the Bible as being a manual that goes along with the "product," which is *you?* The Book and you are meant to go together, to be inseparable. Both were brought into being by the same breath of God (Gen. 2:7; II Tim. 3:16). The Bible was given *for* you, to go *with* you. This is clearly God's design.

When God put man, His supreme creation, on this earth, He did not leave him there without instructions from his Creator. In the garden of Eden, it was by audible *conversation*. Then, for all centuries, there would be *Spirit to spirit communion*. But another method of God to give instructions to mankind on how to live (and how to die!) was by human *written language*. And so, over a period of one and a half millenniums God caused a Book to be written, by men breathed upon by the Holy Spirit, the Book which He intended was to "go with" man.

Its Author urges us to read the *entire* Book *carefully,* and to follow its directions, if we would get the greatest pleasure out of life. Here are some of the important things it writes about:

A. *Our Maker.*

Most of the Bible was written to tell about our Creator and Saviour: who He is, what kind of heart He has, what He does.

Human words cannot fully describe Him, for He is infinite and eternal in all His attributes. But in picture words (even "Spirit" — *wind* — and "Christ" — *anointed* — are picture words), and in men's testimonies of their experiences with Him, and in records of His dealings with men, we are given all that is needed to know of our Maker. He is Wonderful, Counselor, Mighty God, Everlasting Father, Prince of Peace. He doeth all things well. Nothing is too hard for Him. In Him all things are held together. He loves man with an infinite love.

B. *Our Destiny.*

In one sense the Bible may be likened to a map, charting a course to heaven. It shows that the way to heaven is a person, Jesus Christ. It also warns of another way, a way of separation from God for rejecting His Son Jesus. That is the road to hell.

C. *Our Present Life.*

The Bible is our instruction book on how to live in this life, with a view to the life beyond. It is a book of deep and infinite truths. But it speaks its vital message of salvation and Christian living in such a way that even a child can respond.

The Bible warns against negligence of things present and apathy toward things to come. It says a man *must* be born again if he is to find lasting and real joy and peace. It tells the unsaved man how to live, by showing him he *cannot* so live as long as he is estranged from God. It tells the saved man how to live by show-

11

ing him the power of the indwelling and filling Holy Spirit. He is to keep all parts clean by the Word: "Wherewithal shall a young man cleanse his way? by taking heed thereto according to thy word" (Ps. 119:9). He is not to abuse body, soul or spirit, but present these to God. For such living, the Bible promises abundant joys and rivers of living water reaching out to the parched needs of men.

The Bible abounds in messages that offer help and healing and repair for our needy souls. When things go wrong in life, we are often prone to by-pass God and go everywhere else first for help. We go to psychiatrists, psychologists, advisers and friends. We take tension pills and talk-yourself-out-of-it potions. We consult God only as a last resort, when we should have run to Him at the first symptoms of trouble. For God is the source of all help for His creation: in Him lies the power to help, and repair, and mend, and redeem!

God is the master mechanic, who knows the machine He has made, and who has a warehouse of replacement parts. Bent, broken, dirty, squeaky, weak, or run-down parts are no problem to Him. When King David acknowledged the wrong of his heart and deed, he confessed his sin, and so could expect a restored and repaired joy and usefulness in God's service: "Restore unto me the joy of thy salvation . . . Then will I teach transgressors thy ways; and sinners shall be converted unto thee" (Ps. 51:12-13).

*　　*　　*

The Bible is the Book of God's heart. It is the Book that God wants us to read, and believe, and obey. It is the Book that gives all the wherewithal of living. It is the only Book that offers a warranty for eternity.

III. The Bible is MANNA for strength.

God would not give us directions for living unless He also gave strength to follow those directions. That strength or energy comes from the spiritual food of His Word. When God directed His people through the wildernesses of Sinai, He fed them daily with manna, so that they would have the physical strength to advance. The Bible itself likens meditation and study of its pages to eating food for the body.

Everyone must eat, to live and grow. Any Israelite on the wilderness journey who refused to eat the manna or the quail supplied by God, perished, for there was no other food. Man can go so long without food, but eventually he will die.

The Bible is our spiritual food for life and for growth. Like Job we should treasure the words of God's mouth more than our necessary food (Job 23:12).

Healthy people eat because they are hungry. Hunger is a sign of health. When we neglect the Bible, it is because we are not hungry for the things of God. Not being hungry, we cannot therefore be healthy, spiritually. And we will not be hungry for God's Word if we do not acknowledge our need of that Word. An honest look into our heart should make us cry out with the psalmist, "My soul breaketh for the longing that it hath unto thy judgments at all times" (Ps. 119:20). That is soul hunger, and it is holy.

Reading and studying the Bible should be the happy pastime of all Christians. Just as the manna was sweet to the taste of God's people, so is the Bible to those who absorb it wholeheartedly. The psalmist experienced this: "How sweet are thy words unto my taste! Yea, sweeter than honey to my mouth! (Ps. 119:103). Jeremiah said, "Thy words were found, and I did eat them; and thy word was unto me the joy and rejoicing of mine heart" (Jer. 15:16a). Ezekiel experienced that even the bitter words of God, involving mourning and woe, are transformed to sweetness when taken into the soul (Ezek. 2:8-3:3).

Manna in the wilderness was a daily gift of God to all His people. The supply was always there for everyone, as long as the people used what God gave. The Bible is God's ever-present gift to us. If we study it today, it will be more attractive to us tomorrow, and still more attractive the next day. God's gifts always increase in the measure of their use.

"Light obeyed increaseth light;
Light rejected bringeth night."

The Bible is truly "angels' food," come down from heaven, spread out on our table in the wilderness (Ps. 78:19-25). Dare we pass by this food?

14

APPROACHING THE BIBLE

Chapter 2

How to Approach the Bible

THE BIBLE is Everyman's book. It is open to the un-schooled and to the doctor of philosophy. Whenever a translation of the Bible is made, the translators avoid technical words and phrases, seeking to make the Book clear to the average reader, and still faithful to the original writings. William Tyndale, who translated the first printed English New Testament (1525), had the laity, like the "boy that driveth the plough," in mind in all his translation work. He wrote once, "I had per-ceaved by experyence, how that it was impossible to stablysh the laye people in any truth, excepte the scripture were playnly layde before their eyes in their mother tonge, that they might se the processe, ordre and meaninge of the texte. . . ."

Bible study is for all, and the procedures for study apply equally to all. For those who are called to special ministries of the Word, there are refinements and exten-sions of the procedures, but the basic approach in Bible study is common to all Christians.

There lies a copy of the Bible on our desk, a veri-table invitation to blessing. It waits to be read, and to be studied. But how should we approach this? Let us consider some basic approaches.

I. TREAT THE BIBLE AS A BOOK.

The Bible is a book to be read. It should be read wholly, not in part; purposefully, not haphazardly; intelligently, not amiss.

The Bible is one book, with the one theme of God's salvation to sinful man by Jesus Christ. Any one part of the Bible should be read with ultimate reference to this grand theme. Otherwise the main point of the writing will be lost.

The Bible is also a library of sixty-six volumes which grew together in the course of the centuries by the guiding hand of God. These sixty-six books are works of literature, and must be read as such. There are prose writings, such as the many historical books; and there are poetical books, like the Psalms. When we are reading prose, we can expect to see plain language recounting the truth. The epistles of the New Testament have their own unique characteristics, and we read them as personal letters revealing the great truths of God and of practical Christian living. When we are reading poetry, we can expect to see much figurative language, teaching the truth.

We should also remember that an author of a book of the Bible composed his work according to normal writing procedures. He had a main purpose in writing, and subordinate ones as well. He brought together many facts, and produced one book. That is what composition is, and we should keep this in mind when we read a book of the Bible. Such an attitude will deter us from doing the author an injustice, such as making conclusions before we have read his *entire* book.

The format of a book of the Bible is also like any other book. There are chapters, which are broken down into paragraphs; then sentences (usually the length of a verse); then words. All Bibles now follow a standard system of chapter divisions (originated by Stephen Langton in 1228) and verse divisions (originated by Robert Stephanus in 1560). Paragraph divisions have never been standardized, but the paragraph unit must always be kept in mind in Bible study. Most modern versions show paragraph divisions by means of some printing device, such as indentation or asterisk.

We have referred to the Bible earlier as a *library* of sixty-six volumes. When we speak of it as one *book,* then its sixty-six parts could rightly be called chapters. Our question here is, are these sixty-six "chapters" arranged in our Bibles in a purposeful pattern? The answer is yes. While there is no unbroken chain of style, plot, etc., from book to book, each writing is located in a particular group. The books of the Bible have been generally grouped according to topic and type of writing. These groups will be identified later in this section. Though there is a general chronological order (from the original creation, Genesis, to the new creation, Revelation), that is not the key to the overall arrangement. However, it is necessary to know the chronological sequence of Bible history in order to appreciate the setting of each book. This applies especially to the Old Testament. The following chart shows the major eras and points of Old Testament history. Master this chart and you will find it easier to remember the setting of each Old Testament book, especially the prophetical books.

Notice where the Old Testament record begins and ends. The period "400 Silent Years" is so-called because no Bible book was written during this period.

Now let us observe how the books have been grouped in the Old Testament, with this historical survey in mind. There are four major groups: Pentateuch (the word means "five-fold vessel," and refers

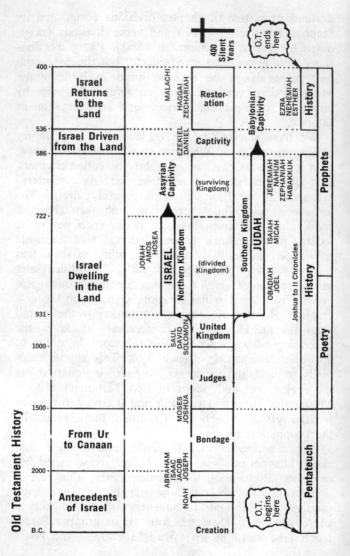

Old Testament History

	400 Silent Years	✝
		O.T. ends here

400 —

Israel Returns to the Land — MALACHI / HAGGAI / ZECHARIAH — Restoration — EZRA NEHEMIAH ESTHER — History

536 —

Israel Driven from the Land — EZEKIEL / DANIEL — Captivity — Babylonian Captivity

586 —

Assyrian Captivity — (surviving Kingdom) — JEREMIAH / NAHUM / ZEPHANIAH / HABAKKUK — Prophets

ISAIAH / MICAH

722 —

JONAH / AMOS / HOSEA

Israel Dwelling in the Land — ISRAEL Northern Kingdom — (divided Kingdom) — Southern Kingdom — JUDAH — Joshua to II Chronicles — History

OBADIAH / JOEL

931 —

SAUL / DAVID / SOLOMON — United Kingdom — Poetry

1000 —

Judges

1500 —

MOSES / JOSHUA

From Ur to Canaan — Bondage

2000 —

ABRAHAM / ISAAC / JACOB / JOSEPH — Pentateuch

Antecedents of Israel — NOAH

B.C. — Creation — O.T. begins here

18

to the five books of Moses, the Books of the Law),
History, Poetry, Prophecy. Note with what period of
history on the historical survey chart these four groups
are identified. There are two groups among the prophetical books, called Major Prophets (the five longer
books of Isaiah to Lamentations) and Minor Prophets
(the twelve shorter books). An easy way to remember
the Old Testament groups is to recall the numbers of
books in each group (notice the symmetrical arrangement):

5	12	5	5	12
PENTATEUCH	HISTORY	POETRY	MAJOR PROPHETS	MINOR PROPHETS
Genesis to Deuteronomy	Joshua to Esther	Job to Songs	Isaiah to Lamentations	Hosea to Malachi
Mainly Narrative		Mainly Reflection	Mainly Oracles	

You will note that there are essentially only three
kinds of content (narrative, reflection, oracles), just as
there are three kinds of New Testament writings (narrative, interpretation, prophecy).

It is the prophetical books of the Old Testament
that are the most difficult to associate with their historical settings, because the names Major Prophets and
Minor Prophets give no clue here. When we read a
prophetical book, we should know to which of the
following three *historical* groups it belongs:

1. *pre-exilic prophets:*
    —prophesying to the northern kingdom (Israel):
      Jonah, Amos, Hosea
    —prophesying to the southern kingdom (Judah):
      Obadiah, Joel, Isaiah, Micah, Jeremiah, Nahum,
      Zephaniah, Habakkuk

19

2. *exilic prophets:* Ezekiel, Daniel
3. *post-exilic prophets:* Haggai, Zechariah, Malachi

Refer to the historical survey chart again and identify each prophet in his place and time.

The New Testament has basically a three-fold arrangement, determined by content:

5	21	1
HISTORY	LETTERS	PROPHECY
4 Gospels Acts	13 Pauline Epistles 8 General Epistles	Revelation
Mainly Narrative	Mainly Interpretation	Mainly Prophecy

When the Old and New Testaments are seen together as one book, which they are, Jesus Christ is the central person. The following outline brings this out:

THE KEY: JESUS

5 Books of Law	12 Historical Books	5 Poetic Books	17 Prophetic Books	4 Gospels	1 Acts	21 Letters	1 Revelation
Revel-ation	Anticipation -types-experiences-prophecies			Manifest-ation	Realization		Coron-ation

This is not to say that every biblical passage is Messianic or Christological, but that all Scripture, since it is the book about God and His world, focuses on the consummation of God's plans concerning this world, and Jesus Christ is the peak of that consummation (Rev. 22).

Let us look a little more into the relationship between the Old and New Testaments. The two testaments are inseparable, and should be treated as such. "The New is in the Old concealed; the Old is in the New revealed." We should not divide what God has joined together. The following diagram shows the intimate relationships of the two testaments.

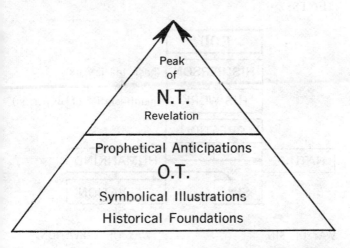

The Old Testament books are the basic books of the pyramid, providing the necessary historical foundations. The Old Testament books are also picture books, filled with symbols, types and illustrative narratives, illustrating the great theological truths enacted and expounded in the New. Also throughout the Old are the many prophetical anticipations of the New. Without the prophecies the supernatural luster of the fulfillments would be erased. So the Old Testament supports, enlightens and anticipates the New, causing the peak of divine revelation—God speaking in His Son (Heb. 1:1-2)—to rise high in all of its glory.

21

Let us bring this discussion around to the practical business of our Bible study. If the Old Testament should be studied because it is so important, what should we look for when we are studying one of its passages? Every passage of the Bible, whether in the Old or New Testament, has something to say about one or more of the following big UNIVERSAL SUBJECTS:

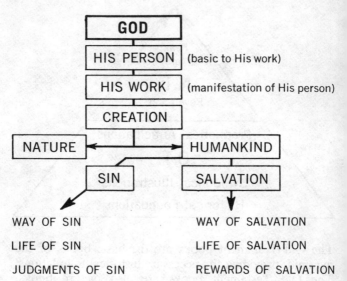

When you study an Old Testament passage, look for these truths. It will amaze you how much you will find. The main thread appearing most often throughout the Bible is that of SALVATION (right-hand side of the diagram). Whether you are studying in the Old or New Testament, you will find the Bringer of Salvation, the Way of Salvation and the People of Salvation to be the same. An Old Testament passage may

22

illustrate an aspect of salvation (e.g., the deliverance of the exodus); or prophesy of it (e.g., Isa. 53); or even state it explicitly (e.g., Gen. 15:6). Whatever it says, and however it says it, should be cherished by the Bible student just as enthusiastically as a New Testament passage of similar teaching.

We have been saying in this section that since the Bible is a book, it should be read and studied as a book. Here are a few other things we should recognize about this book as we read it. They are things we can expect in a writing of this sort:

1. *The personalities* of the authors are different, so style and vocabulary differ from book to book.

2. *The general place* of writing needs to be recognized, for customs and cultures may explain actions and words foreign to our part of the world.

3. *The perspective* of the author, as to time, is not static. He may skip over periods (as in prophetic "gaps"), or he may backtrack in descriptions (as in historical accounts).

4. *The progression* in revelation is to be expected from author to author, in view of the centuries-span of the entire writing of the Bible. God did not give a *full* revelation of truth to the first writer of a book of the Bible.

II. TREAT THE BIBLE AS A UNIQUE BOOK.

The Bible is like any other book as to its literary composition, but there the similarities end. Someone has said, "Treat the Bible like any other book and you will find that it is not like any other book." The world has never seen a book like the Bible. The Bible is such a book as man could not have written if he would, and would not have written if he could. Robert G.

Bratcher, translator of the widely acclaimed *Today's English Version,* gave this testimony of his experience with the New Testament as he worked over its words and sentences:

> The most rewarding moments came at those times when one really felt oneself to be 'in tune' with the sacred authors—where one was swept up by the beauty, dignity and eloquence of the authors, and felt moved by the same divine power that moved them to write as they did. These were rare and precious moments I would not exchange for any other experiences I have had.

What makes the Bible such a unique book? Here are some answers:

A. *It is God's only written communication to man.*

In a miraculous way God inspired men to write His message, telling the world that He *wants* to save them and that He *can* save them.

The Bible is God's personal love letter to us. When we open its pages, should we regard it any less than we do a letter from our beloved? He who sees the Bible as a personal "love-letter" from his Creator and also Saviour will learn much in his Bible study.

B. *It is completely trustworthy.*

This Book makes fantastic claims and predictions, and still it remains trustworthy, because it was written by God. "Scripture cannot be broken" (John 10:35). The absolute Word of the absolute God is absolute authority for life. If God cannot be trusted, who can? The Bible is not a book of "cunningly devised fables," but of a "sure word of prophecy" (II Pet. 1:16, 19). No other book has such a distinction.

C. *It is inexhaustible.*

The Bible is like a mine of treasures, infinitely deep, always inviting the student to a second chamber, after he has spent time in the first. This was Augustine's reflection in writing his son in A.D. 412: "Such is the depth of the Christian Scriptures that even if I were attempting to study them and nothing else from early boyhood to decrepit old age, with the utmost leisure, the most unwearied zeal, and talents greater than I have, I would still daily be making progress in discovering their treasures."

We must never expect to exhaust the full meaning of the Bible, because it speaks of infinite, eternal and mysterious truths, not fully grasped by our finite minds. Moody said, "Men who know the Bible best find it ever new."

III. APPROACH THE BIBLE WITH RIGHT ATTITUDES.

Thus far in this chapter we have been talking about our *recognition* of the Bible—that it is to be read as a *book,* and as a *unique* book. But our approach to Bible study involves much more than this. Demanded of us are various attitudes, without which Bible study can be very barren and even inaccurate. Here are some of those necessary attitudes:

A. *Reverence*

The Bible is the book of the words of God. God has not chosen to record His will permanently in any other writing. How important for us to revere its pages of truth, as it tells about the God whom we worship. Someone has said, "Access to the inmost sanctuary of the Holy Scriptures is granted only to those who come to worship." Of course we do not worship the Book, but the God of the Book.

Robert Evans tells of meeting an old man in bombed-out Warsaw after World War II, who had owned and cherished one page of a Bible all his life, but he was not sure that it was from the Bible. "I have read this page again and again all my life," he told Evans. "I thought it was from the Bible, but I was never sure. There is something different about it—this I know. But I have always wondered what comes on the next page." And then he wept, as Evans let him see and handle for the first time in his life an entire Bible, page by page.

B. *Dependence*

We need to see our *need* of Bible study, or incentive and inspiration will be lacking. Wilbur M. Smith says, "If we could come to an hour in our lives when before God we would say that Bible study *must* be given a definite, paramount place in our lives, every day, because we realize that we *absolutely need it,* then, no matter what interruptions are experienced, or what might be our immediate reactions to such study, we would keep at it persistently, because we knew we needed it."[1]

Convinced of our need of studying the Bible, and knowing also our inability to understand it without help, we should depend on the Holy Spirit who indwells us (Rom. 8:9) and who was given to guide us into all the truth (John 16:13). We must study the Bible under His influence, for, as D. L. Moody once said, "The Bible without the Holy Spirit is a sun-dial by moonlight."

C. *Desire*

It is one thing to know that we need to study the Bible. It is another thing to desire to study it. Such

1. Wilbur M. Smith, *Profitable Bible Study* (Boston: W. A. Wilde Company, 1939), p. 11.

a desire is not forced, but should come naturally to the one who knows the Author personally, and loves His fellowship. This is what Peter had in mind when he wrote, "Desire the sincere milk of the word . . . if so be ye have tasted that the Lord is gracious" (I Peter 2:2-3). The book that first appeared dull to a young woman reading it suddenly became a fascinating story at a later reading, simply because in the meantime she had fallen in love with its author.

And if we desire to study the Bible, we will not shun the toil and the sweat which fruitful Bible study demands. G. Campbell Morgan wrote this: "The Bible yields its treasures to honest toil more readily than does any other serious literature. The Bible never yields to indolence."

D. *Exactness*

Whether we are studying a large movement of the Bible or a small detail, we should always strive to be exact and accurate. Since the original autographs were infallible, and since our present Bible text has been carefully preserved, it behooves us to study the Bible with as much care and methodicalness as can be humanly mustered. This is another attitude in Bible study that honors God and produces blessed benefits.

E. *Receptivity*

This is the attitude of submission and moldability. We approach the Bible not to do something to it, but to let it do something to us. With an open heart and mind, we are prepared to understand the Scriptures (cf. Luke 24:45).

27

ABSORBING THE BIBLE

Chapter 3

How to Read the Bible

THE BIBLE was written to be read. An unread Bible is like food that is refused, an unopened love letter, a buried sword, a road map not studied, a gold mine not worked. It has been aptly said, "A book is a book only when it is in the hands of a reader; the rest of the time it is an artifact." If you have been neglecting reading your Bible determine now to make Bible reading a vital part of your life.

Notice that this chapter is about *reading* the Bible, while the next chapter is about *studying* the Bible. This is the natural order. It is amazing how many Christians want to be Bible *students* without being Bible *readers*. Years ago, Richard Moulton, a Bible scholar in his own right, made this comment:

> We have done almost everything that is possible with these Hebrew and Greek writings. We have overlaid them, clause by clause, with exhaustive commentaries; we have translated them, revised the translations, and quarrelled over the revisions; we have discussed authenticity and inspiration, and suggested textual history with the aid of colored type; we have mechanically divided the whole into chapters and verses, and sought texts to memorize and quote; we have epitomized into handbooks and ex-

28

tracted school lessons . . . There is yet one thing left to do with the Bible: *simply to read it.*[1]

I. SOME PRACTICAL SUGGESTIONS

The two most commonly asked questions about Bible reading are, When should I read the Bible? and, How should I read it? Of course there is no rigid set of answers to such questions, but some practical suggestions may help you in your own situation.

A. *Time*

Where does one *find* time to read the Bible? Free time is so scarce for most Christians that it is never found. So we must *take* time to read the Bible, scheduling it at a regular time, if possible, in each day. Someone has said, "We ought to have a Medo-Persian hour—an unchangeable hour for our Bible study." This is not an impossible nor unreasonable demand, seeing how easily we can schedule the daily reading of the newspaper and the weekly reading of periodicals. The time chosen for Bible reading should be when the body and mind are fresh and not weary, with no pressures or distractions from without. There is no substitute for being alone with God and His Word.

Don't wait for an opportune time to begin reading your Bible. Begin *now*. It is very true for Bible reading that the biggest waste of time is the time wasted in getting started.

B. *Passage*

The length of the passage you read will vary from time to time. One chapter is an average length; sometimes, especially in the deeper doctrinal portions of the Bible, you should meditate on no more than a

1. Richard G. Moulton, *A Short Introduction to the Literature of the Bible* (Boston: D. C. Heath and Co., 1901), pp. iii-iv. Italics mine.

paragraph or even a verse. Some have chosen to read through the Bible in a year, which involves three to four chapters a day (there are 1189 chapters in the Bible). A more practical plan is to read through the Bible in three years (about one chapter a day). See a suggested 3-year schedule at the back of this book. In determining the length of the passage to be read, remember that you want to read that which can be read *thoroughly*. The important thing is not how many times you've gone through the Bible, but whether the Bible has gone through you. George Mueller's rule as to the length of the passage read each time was this: "I read until I come to a verse upon which I can lean my whole weight, and then stop."

In reading the Bible, it is good to alternate between the New and Old Testaments. For example, read first a Gospel (N.T.); then Genesis (O.T.); then Acts or an epistle (N.T.); then Exodus (O.T.), and so forth.

A chapter from Proverbs and Psalms could be added to each daily reading, for the practical and worshipful aspects of daily living. (Note that Proverbs has thirty-one chapters, one for each day of the month.)

C. *Versions*

Which version of the Bible should you read? The answer is: one version, *and* other versions.

1. *one version*—You should concentrate mostly on one version, letting its words become a part of you, as you meditate on them. For retaining verses by way of memorization, this version should be the King James, for this is the one standard version for memory work.

2. *other versions*—The value of reading other modern versions cannot be overemphasized. Try reading, for example, the gospel of John in one of the modern versions listed below. You will see things you never

saw before, because the translation is fresher and different from what you are accustomed to reading. History has shown that the production of Bible versions in the simple speech of everyday life has greatly encouraged reading of the Bible by the laity.[2] Another value of comparing a particular Bible passage from version to version is that a fuller representation of the original writing, in all of its color and shades of meaning, is seen.

Here are some good Bible versions, published since 1900, listed in chronological order. Those marked with an asterisk are either very free or expanded renderings:

Complete Bible:

American Standard Version . . . . (1901)
Revised Standard Version . . . . (1952)
Berkeley Version . . . . (1959)
Amplified Bible* . . . . (1965)
New English Bible . . . . (1970)
New American Standard Bible . . . . (1971)
The Living Bible* . . . . (1971)

New Testament Only:

Charles B. Williams *(The New Testament In the Language of the People)* . . . . . . (1937)
J. B. Phillips* *(The New Testament In Modern English)* . . . . (1958)
Kenneth Wuest* *(The New Testament: An Expanded Translation)* . . . . (1961)
William F. Beck* *(The New Testament In the Language of Today)* . . . . (1963)
Today's English Version . . . . (1966)

2. The paperback New Testament, *Today's English Version,* is a recent example of this. Initially intended for people with a limited proficiency in English, this version has become popular with all groups and ages, including housewives, college students and professional people.

D. *Editions*

Versions of the Bible are printed in various editions, representing a wide spectrum of format, quality and price. You can help your personal Bible reading immeasurably by the right choice of a Bible edition. Use a Bible whose print is large and clear, with generous space in the margins for notations. Those with the editors' marginal notes, including cross references, are of much help, provided they stimulate rather than hinder personal, independent study. Paragraph format, and a text that reads across the entire page, will also enhance your reading (e.g., Williams.) Also use a Bible whose paper is conducive to ink or pencil notations. You will never regret any investment you make in a good edition of the Bible.

II. WHAT BIBLE READING REALLY INVOLVES

Have you ever read an entire page in a book unaware of what you were reading? If so, you know that it is possible to *read without having read!*

The eye activity of reading, basic as it is, is not enough in Bible reading. More activities are involved, which are described below. They are listed under the four headings, Reading, Reflection, Recording and Response. Let us look at each of these.

A. *Reading*

This is the eye activity. How can we help ourselves to become keener observers, and avoid the pitfall of the heavy eye?

1. *Read aloud.* It will amaze you how new vistas are opened as you hear your own voice speaking words and sentences you may never have voiced before. When you read, read interpretatively, with meaning and feeling. The blessed effects of reading aloud from the Psalms are described by William Law, in the classic

work, *A Serious Call to the Devout and Holy Life:*

"You are to consider this [reading aloud] of a psalm as a necessary beginning of your devotions, as something that is to awaken all that is good and holy within you, that is to call your spirits to their proper duty, to set you in your best posture towards heaven, and tune all the powers of your soul to worship and adoration.

"For there is nothing that so clears a way for your prayers, nothing that so disperses dullness of heart, nothing that so purifies the soul from poor and careless passions, nothing that so opens heaven, or carries your heart so near to it, as these songs of praise."[3]

2. *Read carefully.* Read alertly, not mechanically. There is a place in Bible study for the quick, cursive reading, but in devotional reading you must read slowly as well as carefully, weighing each word, and even the punctuation. It is possible to tour a country so fast that one does not really see the land. Such a person has been called a "tripper," in contrast to the traveler, who journeys slowly to absorb not only the sights, but also the sounds and the aromas. Study the Bible as a traveler who is not pushed by any impulse to dart off to the next stop. Gaze long across its fields of truths. Climb its mountains of vision. Cross its valleys of trial. Cool yourself in its streams of inspiration. Take in all you can as the Holy Spirit guides you through its many halls of instruction.

Train your eyes to read carefully. It is very true today that there is much crooked *thinking* because there is much crooked *seeing.*

Each word in the Bible has a function. Always seek to learn what that is. This may be slow going,

3. William Law, *A Serious Call to the Devout and Holy Life* (London: Aldine House, 1898), p. 219.

but it is necessary. A butterfly covers more ground, but a bee gathers more honey. Be like the bee.

3. *Read repeatedly.* Return often to the beginning of the passage. One thrust of the spade does not unearth all the gems of the Bible's mine. Don't ever conclude that you have exhausted the meaning of a verse when it becomes familiar to you. John Bunyan said that "old truths are always new to us if they come to us with the smell of Heaven upon them."

4. *Read peripherally.* Peripheral vision is seeing the surroundings while the eye is focused straight ahead. Good auto drivers and football quarterbacks must have excellent peripheral vision. So in Bible study you should keep your eyes open to the surrounding context of the words you are reading. This can be one of the best single study aids in understanding the passage.

B. *Reflection*

When God speaks to us, we should stand still and consider what He is saying. In Bible reading, reflection is the mind and heart at work, thinking over what the eyes have seen. That is quite different from merely seeing with the eye, which is what someone has labelled "retinizing." Reflection in Bible reading should have the intensity of meditation, whereby the soul has the desire and intention of obeying God's Word. "Thou shalt meditate therein day and night, that thou mayest observe to do according to all that is written therein" (Joshua 1:8).

How should we reflect on the Scriptures? Here are some suggestions:

1. *Reflect purposefully.* The psalmist had a purpose in hiding God's Word in his heart: that he might not sin against God (Ps. 119:11). The Berean Christians had a purpose in examining the Scriptures daily: that they might know the truth (Acts 17:11).

Bible meditation should not be haphazard, or piece-meal. If you want to keep a fire burning in your soul, don't scatter its fuel. Also, recall the "seed-pickers" of Paul's day who flitted here and there, picking up bits of talk about any subject, arriving at no good conclusions. (Paul was falsely accused of being a seed-picker in Acts 17:18, where the word is translated "babbler" in the Authorized Version.) Reading only isolated verses, out of context, and expanding them according to personal whims, is a dangerous practice, for, as Samuel Coleridge has said, such truths "lie bed-ridden in the dormitory of the soul, side by side with the most despised and exploded errors." It is as foolish and fruitless to read the Bible without purpose as it is to search about a room looking for nothing in particular.

What are your purposes as you meditate on the Scriptures? Do you want to know God more intimately, and glorify Him? Do you want to know more about yourself? Do you want to grow strong spiritually? Do you want to know God's will, hear a word of comfort, receive a challenge? Then reflect purposefully!

2. *Reflect imaginatively.* This is not difficult, if you are willing to put yourself into the situation of the Bible passage. Taste and feel every word you read. The great translator, Miles Coverdale, wrote to a friend once, "Now I begyne to taste of Holy Schryptures; now (honour be to God) I am sett to the most swete smell of holy lettyres . . . ."

If the passage is narrative, visualize the setting. Take this verse as an example: "He ordered the crowd to sit down on the ground. Then he took the seven loaves, gave thanks to God, broke them, and gave them to his disciples to distribute to the crowd; and the disciples did so" (Mark 8:6, *Today's English Version*). Try meditating on this verse imagining yourself as one of the crowd, or as one of the disciples. Such exercise will give birth to many blessed insights.

If the passage is doctrine or exhortation, put yourself in the middle of it, for after all, are you not the pupil being taught? Try this with Colossians 2:3: "He (Christ) is the key that opens all the hidden treasures of God's wisdom and knowledge" (TEV). Imagine how rich you are in Christ!

Reflect imaginatively also on passages that do not pertain to you now as a Christian. Do you shudder when you meditate on verses like Luke 13:27-28: "I know you not . . . depart from me . . . there shall be weeping and gnashing of teeth"? Do such verses cause you to exclaim "There am I but for the grace of God"? Do they challenge you concerning the hundreds of thousands of souls passing away daily into a Christless eternity? Years ago a seminary graduating-class heard these words from the speaker: "Would that upon the naked, palpitating heart of each one of you might be laid one red hot coal of God Almighty's wrath!"

Something is bound to stir within your soul the moment you begin to reflect imaginatively as you read the Bible.

3. *Reflect humbly.* The Word you are reading is the *holy* Word of the *holy* God. God is bigger than His Book. As someone has said, "Behind and beneath the Bible, above and beyond the Bible, is the God of the Bible." It should humble you to think that this Holy One, who is also the Almighty One, has spoken to you in the Bible, and has given you the blessed privilege to read it, and so to listen to Him.

When you open your Bible to read it and reflect on it, remember that this is *The Holy Bible,* a title given to no other book in the world. The translators

of the King James Version recognized this, as borne
out by these words contained in their introduction:

> The original thereof from heaven, not from earth;
> the inditer: the Holy Spirit, not the wit of the
> apostles or prophets;
> the penmen: those that were sanctified from the
> womb and endowed with a principal
> portion of God's Spirit;
> the matter: verity, purity, uprightness;
> the form: God's Word, God's testimony,
> God's oracles, the Word of Truth,
> the Word of Salvation, the Light of
> Understanding;
> the stableness of persuasion: repentance from
> dead works, newness of life, holi-
> ness, peace and joy in the Holy
> Ghost.
>
> Happy is the man that delighteth in this Holy
> Word, and thrice happy he that meditateth in it
> day and night.

4. *Reflect prayerfully.* If you reflect humbly, you will
reflect prayerfully, for the contrite heart craves to speak
to the One on whom it depends. The greatest prayer
ever prayed by a man in connection with the Scriptures
is the 119th psalm. Study this psalm carefully to
learn how to reflect prayerfully on the Word. One
example is cited here: "Open thou mine eyes, that I
may behold wondrous things out of thy law" (Ps.
119:18).

> Within that awful volume lies
> The mystery of mysteries!
> Happiest they of human race,
> To whom God has granted grace
> To read, to fear, to hope, to pray,
> To lift the latch, and force the way;

37

And better that they'd ne'er been born,
Who read to doubt, or read to scorn.

Sir Walter Scott (1771-1832)

5. *Reflect patiently*. Patience in any phase of life is priceless. The great naturalist Fabre always referred to his two best instruments as "time" and "patience." Patience on the part of young Clyde Tombaugh is what led him finally to discover the planet Pluto. After astronomers calculated a probable orbit for this "suspected" heavenly body which they had never seen, Tombaugh took up the search in March, 1929. *Time* magazine records the investigation:

> He examined scores of telescopic photographs, each showing tens of thousands of star images, in pairs under the blink comparator, or dual microscope. It often took three days to scan a single pair. It was exhausting, eye-cracking work—in his own words, 'brutal tediousness.' And it went on for months. Star by star, he examined 20 million images. Then on February 18, 1930, as he was blinking a pair of photographs in the constellation Gemini, 'I suddenly came upon the image of Pluto!' It was the most dramatic astronomic discovery in nearly 100 years, and it was made possible by the patience of an American.[4]

The New Testament makes many references to the gem of Christian patience. Patience is surely a requirement in the meditative process of reading God's Word. In fact the phrase "wait on the Lord" can be applied to meditation. Reflection requires time and concentration, and the good Bible student will give both. For his patience he will be rewarded, as was the astronomer Tombaugh, with the pleasure and excitement of dis-

4. *Time Magazine,* April 1, 1966, p. 10.

covering stars of divine truth which he had never seen before.

The call to reflection in Bible reading is expressed in Samuel's plain words to Saul, "Stand thou still a while, that I may show thee the word of God" (I Sam. 9:27).

C. *Recording*

Unless you are gifted with a photographic memory, it is impossible for you to retain for very long all the things you see in a productive study of a biblical passage. This is because the Bible contains so much, and because there is a divine activity of ever-intensifying illumination going on in your mind as you meditate on this Word. There is no comparable study situation in all the world.

What can you do to retain what you see? JOT IT DOWN! Jot it down on a piece of paper, and also in the margins of your Bible. Underline words and phrases that strike fire in your soul. Record your observations as you see them, and your mind will be released to look for more. Professor Agassiz of Harvard said, "The pencil is one of the best eyes." Not only does recording provide a permanent record of what has been observed in Bible study; it also initiates other lines of inquiry.

This author has written much about the process of recording in the book *Independent Bible Study.*[5] Hear what the Bible scholar Wilbur M. Smith has to say about recording, quoted at length because of its pertinence:

> We are now going to suggest something that so few Bible teachers seem to find it necessary to recommend, and yet, after years of experience, we

5. Moody Press, 1963.

believe it is one of the most essential aspects of personal, devotional Bible study. We refer to the making of notes. People can so easily read a page of the Bible and then give some time for meditating upon it, and actually think that they have profited by the half hour they have spent with the Word; but, if you were to ask them what they gleaned from the Word, that day, they would frequently find it difficult to put their fingers on any one rich truth that they had obtained. Another has well said: 'The Bible study that is done in one's head is very apt to get out of one's head . . . . Our heads lose very fast what goes through them, and if we trust to retaining by our memories what we do in our Bible study, we shall lose most of it.' If, however, each young Christian would have a little notebook and actually write down, morning by morning, what the Lord gives out of the verse he or she is meditating upon, it would be found that thoughts would be clarified, the profit derived from Bible study would be greatly increased, and a definite record of the things that the Holy Spirit has taught from day to day, and from week to week, would be had in permanent form. If one does not care to use a notebook, then let one use the margin of his Bible, providing it is a wide margin, and providing it will take ink . . . . The author knows of nothing that will so encourage careful reading of, and sincere meditation upon, the Word of God, delivering us from the great temptation to vagueness and indefiniteness, as a *recording* of what we have found from day to day, in our private notebook, or diary, or in the margins of our Bibles.[6]

For your devotional reading of the Bible, here are some suggested things to record:

1. What is the main point of this passage? Determining such main themes is basic to understanding the

6. *Op. cit.,* pp. 65-67.

various smaller parts of the passage. In this connection also choose a verse in the passage that strikes you as being a key verse. Every passage will have such a verse; some passages may yield more than one golden text.

2. What do other portions of the Bible say that relates to some of these truths? A Bible with cross-references will help here; your acquaintance with the Bible in general will also help. For cross-reference study, a concordance will be handy.

3. What in the passage is difficult to understand; and what problems, if any, appear? Further reading may provide the answers. Reference to commentaries and other outside helps will aid you in a more complete analytical study.[7]

4. How does this apply to my own life? There are two kinds of applications involving me: manward (I and my fellowmen) and Godward (I and God).

D. *Response*

All Bible study by a Christian, whether of a devotional or analytical nature, demands personal response. We are to practise what we read and reflect upon. This is the will in action. The Word was given to storm that will. In our devotional reading of the Bible we should always be looking for examples to follow, errors to avoid, sins to confess, duties to perform, promises to claim, and prayers to echo. Let us consider three major responses which God looks for in our hearts whenever we read the Bible.

1. *Responding with confession.* Since the Bible is the Word of a holy God to people who sin, it is always searching out and exposing that sin. The Word cuts

7. *The Wycliffe Bible Commentary,* edited by Charles F. Pfeiffer and Everett F. Harrison (Chicago: Moody Press, 1962), is a highly recommended one-volume commentary.

as a sword to the very inmost recesses of our being, where it "judges the desires and thoughts of men's hearts. There is nothing that can be hid from God" (Heb. 4:12, TEV). Whenever we read the Bible, it should always be with a heart that acknowledges its sin, and confesses it to God. Then the channel is cleared for further communication with God, and the blessings of Bible reading begin to accrue.

2. *Responding in faith.* Faith involves every part of our Christian life, including our Bible reading. If we do not read the Bible believingly, we lose out utterly. Hebrews 4:2 makes this very clear: "For unto us was the gospel preached, as well as unto them: but the word preached did not profit them, not being *mixed with faith* in them that heard it."

3. *Responding by obedience.* When we obey God's Word, we are demonstrating where our faith rests, and how strong it is. We may not always understand God's ways, but we must always walk in His steps. A dear old woman of deep faith was chided once by an unbeliever concerning her implicit obedience to God. "I suppose if you thought the Lord was telling you to jump through a stone wall, you would jump." To that challenge her reply was simply, "If the Lord told me to jump through a wall, it would be my business to jump, and it would be His business to make the hole."

*　　*　　*　　*

When you read the Bible, always be sure you are *really* reading it. Alert your eyes to see (Reading); stir up your mind to consider (Reflection); write down your observations (Recording); and practise what you read (Response).

ANALYZING THE BIBLE

Chapter 4

Browsing Through a Book

IN THE LAST CHAPTER we discussed Bible *reading*. Beginning with this chapter our attention is centered about the more extensive exercise of Bible *study*. It is true that to read the Bible thoroughly, as described in the last chapter, is to study the Bible. But there is a difference between devotional reading and analytical study, in kind if not in intensity. Every Christian should engage in both activities. He should have his devotions, when his soul is especially scrutinized; and he should work at Bible study, when the Bible text is especially scrutinized.

Where does one begin in Bible study? The correct order is always this: first the whole (e.g., a book of the Bible), then the parts (chapter by chapter). Here are other ways to state this rule:

FIRST	THEN
Image the whole	Execute the parts
Survey study	Analytical study
Skyscraper view	Ground level tour
Panoramic sweep	Microscopic focus

There are two main reasons for this order of *survey before analysis*. These are:

1. To see each part in its intended *emphasis*. Prior survey is a check on the two extremes of overemphasizing or minimizing the point of any one part of Scripture.

2. To see each part in its *relation* to the other parts. Knowing one's bearing in the forest of many facts is a tremendous help in Bible study. This is illustrated by an experience of Charles Lindbergh. On one of his early flights he lost a valuable instrument overboard. He watched it fall and land in the dense fields below. Later he landed a smaller plane in the general vicinity, and scoured the area by foot in search of the instrument, but to no avail. He resorted to a simple expedient. Taking off his coat, he spread it on a bush, and returned to the air. From the air he saw both the coat and the instrument, and he made some mental notes of relationship and bearing. Landing again, he walked to the coat, but still could not find the instrument. So he moved the coat to another bush, and repeated the sighting from the air. With this additional bearing he was able finally to locate the instrument.

Many questions on the interpretation of a verse in the Bible are answered when the location of the verse in the book, with reference to its context, is recognized.

The correct order of Bible study, then, is this: first, we should have in view the entire Bible as a whole; second, we should choose one book of the sixty-six and survey it; third, we should analyze each part (e.g., each chapter) of that book. The first of these three studies, survey of the whole Bible, we have already referred to in chapter 2. You might want to refer back to this section (pages 15-20) for a review of this panoramic sweep of the whole Bible. In this chapter we will make a survey study of one book of the Bible, namely Acts. The chapters that follow are devoted to the analytical studies of a chapter, a verse, a word and a topic. The Scripture passages for these studies are from different books of the Bible. Of necessity the treatment in each chapter of this book cannot be exhaustive. Rather, it is suggestive of a pattern you should follow in your own personal Bible study of other books of the Bible. *Study* the Bible *thoroughly,* and you will *thoroughly enjoy* it!

SURVEY OF THE BOOK OF ACTS

I. HISTORICAL BACKGROUND

Learning the historical background of a book of the Bible is the first step of survey study. Some of this can be learned from the text of the book itself. You will usually want to refer to an outside source for other help concerning this, before studying the text.

A. *Author*

Read Acts 1:1, and compare it with Luke 1:1-4. From this it should be clear that Luke wrote Acts, even though his name does not appear in the text of Acts.

B. *Date*

Note from the last chapter of Acts that the last event to be recorded is the imprisonment of Paul in Rome. This took place around A.D. 61. From all appearances Luke wrote Acts at this time, or very soon thereafter. Since the opening event of Acts, the ascension of Jesus, took place in A.D. 30, the book describes the first three decades of the witness of the Gospel. Keep this in mind as you study Acts.

C. *The Place of Acts in the New Testament*

Each book of the Bible serves a specific function among the sixty-six. A book would not be in the canon of the Bible if it did not make its own contribution to the corpus of Scripture. Let us see what Acts contributes to the New Testament.

First, observe how Acts is related to the Gospel of Luke. Read again Luke 1:1-4 and Acts 1:1-5. Acts 1:1 says that Luke's Gospel records what Jesus *began*

46

to do and teach, in His earthly ministry, suggesting that Acts records what He *continued* to do and teach, through the Holy Spirit. So Acts is the historical sequel to the narrative of the gospels. In the gospels Christ gives His literal body as a sacrifice for men; in Acts He begins to form His spiritual body, the Church, which is comprised of all who accept His sacrifice.

Acts is also the background and attestation of the messages of the epistles. This is seen in the fact that Paul, who wrote at least 13 of the 21 epistles, is a main character of Acts, his conversion being a highlight of the book. (Read chapter 9 at this time.) Epistles written by others (e.g., Peter and John) have their setting in the Christian communities and churches of the Book of Acts. In fact even the seven churches of the Book of Revelation have their origins in Acts. So Acts is truly a pivotal book in the New Testament.

D. *The Purposes of Acts*

After you have made a survey of Acts, you will have seen the main purposes of its writing. It will not inhibit your own original study, however, to identify some of those purposes at this time.

First, there was the need to record the acts of the Holy Spirit, concerning the church's birth, establishment, scattering and extension. (Recall that the gospels were written to record the acts of Jesus, in His earthly life.) Second, there was the purpose of vindicating the stand of the new Christian community. Persecution against the church was shown to be based on false charges, whether religious or political. (Read Acts 4 for an example.) Third, Acts was written to edify believers of all ages who would read its pages. No book of the Bible gives greater incentive for the witness of the Gospel than does the Book of Acts. It is truly a thrilling, contemporary challenge to every servant of God.

II. SURVEY PROCESS

Now let us get to the heart of the Bible study process, involving the biblical text. All Bible study is a progression from obscurity to sight.

Stated in other ways, the progression is: from first impressions, to repeated impressions, to enduring impressions; or, from the random and indefinite, to the organized and defined. The key to advance is: READ and READ and READ. Obviously there is no shortcut in Bible study. In fact, what serious student would seek a shortcut, and miss some treasures on paths so avoided? In your personal study of the Bible don't become impatient or discouraged if you do not seem to be making enough headway. If you are diligently reading the text and letting it soak into your heart and mind as rain is absorbed by the earth, you can claim the promise of Isaiah 55:10-11 that God's Word will not return unto Him as void. Count on the Spirit to lead you from obscurity to sight.

A. *First Reading*

Our first exercise is to read through the twenty-eight chapters of Acts, not slowly, in one sitting if possible. We might call this "browsing through the book," which is the title of this chapter. This is to get the "feel" of the book, and to see the highlights from the start. We shouldn't yield to the temptation to read slowly and to tarry over particular passages. For this reading it is very helpful to read from a colloquial modern-speech version, such as the *Berkeley Version*.

After the reading we should write down a list of our initial impressions. Such impressions might include 1) the persistent opposition of the enemies of the

48

Gospel (e.g., chapters 3-7); 2) the faith and courage of the Christians (e.g., Stephen, chapter 7); 3) the triumph of the church in every instance (e.g., the impotence of the Sanhedrin in prohibiting Peter and John to preach, 4:18-23); 4) the many miracles (e.g., 7:8); 5) the advance of the gospel geographically and nationally (e.g., 13:3ff.); 6) the prominent part of the Holy Spirit in the narrative; 7) the many sermons in the early part of Acts (e.g., 2:14ff.) and defenses of Paul in the last of Acts (e.g., one in each of the chapters 22-26); and 8) the many travels of Paul to reach new cities with the gospel (chapters 13-21).

Just one reading of Acts is an inspiration in itself. But we must go on to more, for we have just begun to behold its treasures.

B. *Second Reading*

In our first reading we were not trying to discover the organization of the book. We read it as one narrative, overlooking even chapter divisions. Now, however, we want to begin to see Luke's plan. Luke, like all writers in composing a book, selected what to include in his work, and what to omit. He brought his materials together according to a plan, and the wonderful Book of Acts is the product. Luke did all this under the inspiration of the Holy Spirit, which gave the book not only veracity but also spiritual depth and beauty. Let us look for clues to the organization of the book, and begin to record these on a survey chart. It is when we have seen the plan and outline of the Book of Acts that we begin to understand more about the power behind the miracle of the first-century church, the overall design of a wise and sovereign God, and what are the really essential things of Christian living.

1. *Chapter titles.* First, let us assign chapter titles to

each chapter (or segment, if the unit is shorter or longer than a chapter). This will help us to fix in our minds something of the "flow" of the book.[1] We will record our chapter titles on a horizontal chart like the following:

Sometimes a unit of study does not begin with the first verse of the chapter. Normally, it is best to proceed as though there were no such exceptions, and pick these up at a later time, when they usually show themselves. We will anticipate this step now, by identifying these exceptions for Acts: 8:1b; 9:32 (in addition to 9:1); 15:36 (instead of 16:1); 18:23 (instead of 19:1); 21:18 (in addition to 21:1).

2. *Emphases by repetition.* The compositional law of proportion gives clues to the organization of a book. Let us look at some of the more important *repeated* items in Acts which would appear very prominent by the time we had read through Acts a second time.

    a. *miracles.* Miracles appear throughout Acts, to the very last chapter. (Read 28:5-6.) This coincides with the purpose of such miracles—that of attesting the message of the apostles to a new group or situation. Throughout Acts the apostles are

1. Chapter titles are vivid single words or short phrases taken directly from the text which serve as clues to the content of the chapter. They are not intended to make a formal outline of the book as such.

always advancing to new situations, hence the miracles to furnish their credentials.

b. *witness*. The word "witness" is the key word of Acts. Referring to an exhaustive concordance,[2] we find that it appears 21 times. Its recurrence is exceeded only in the Gospel of John, where it appears 22 times. A key verse for Acts is 1:8: "But ye shall receive power, after that the Holy Ghost is come upon you: and ye shall be witnesses unto me both in Jerusalem, and in all Judea, and in Samaria, and unto the uttermost part of the earth." The idea of witness itself gives no clue as to any divisions in the organization of Acts, for the Christians continue to witness throughout the book. But the geography of that witness is a definite clue, clearly showing three areas of witness, fulfilled in the order of Jesus' prophecy: 1) Jerusalem, 2) Judea and Samaria, 3) uttermost part of the earth. At some place in the course of our study we would observe that Jerusalem is the center of the witness of chapters 1-7; at 8:1b the church, excluding the apostles, "were all scattered abroad throughout the regions of Judea and Samaria"; and at 13:1 begins the first thrust of the witness of the gospel to "foreign" lands, the "uttermost" parts of the Roman Empire. So we make this geographical outline of "witness" for our survey chart of Acts:

1	8:1b	13:1 28
JERUSALEM	JUDEA & SAMARIA	UTTERMOST PARTS

2. For example, James Strong, *The Exhaustive Concordance of the Bible* (New York: Abingdon Press, 1890).

As we proceed in our study we will observe that the three divisions noted above are the three main parts of Acts with respect to other topics as well.

c. *Jew, Gentile.* Acts refers often to the Jews (mainly under the name Israel) and Gentiles. A comparative study in an exhaustive concordance will show that references to Israel appear mostly in the first part of the book, while the Gentiles are brought into the limelight especially after chapter 8. This is because the church in Acts is shown to move from a constituency mainly of Jews to one that included Gentiles as well. Chapters 10 and 11 are the key chapters pointing out this transition. Read these chapters at this time. At 13:1, where Paul's missionary party begins its evangelical invasion of cities throughout the Roman Empire, the gospel is presented as a universal gospel. This study might be shown on a chart thus (note that we are using the junctions 8:1b and 13:1 which appeared in our study on "witness"):

1:1	8:1b	13:1 28
JEWISH PERIOD	TRANSITION	GENTILE PERIOD
OLD TESTAMENT HERITAGE JEWISH AUDIENCE GENTILE WORLD		UNIVERSAL GOSPEL

d. *Peter, Paul.* The study of persons in any historical book of the Bible will often give clues to the organization of the book. In Acts Peter is definitely *the* leading apostle of chapters 1-7, while Paul is the leading person of chapters 13-

52

28. In the transitional section, chapters 8-12, the four main persons are Peter, Philip, Barnabas and Paul, with Peter still the more active person in the account. We should record this on our survey chart also.

1 PETER	8:1b Philip-Barnabas Peter-Paul	13:1 PAUL 28
ACTS OF PETER		ACTS OF PAUL

e. *the church.* The church is another key subject of Acts, the word itself appearing 22 times in the book. The church is the agent used by God to be a witness of the gospel. An extensive title for Acts might be, *The Gospel In Action By the Holy Spirit Through the Church.* Following the three-fold outline of Acts given in the above descriptions, Acts shows: The Church Established (1-7); The Church Scattered (8-12); The Church Extended (13-28). The church was born on Pentecost, when the disciples were gathered in Jerusalem (1:12; 2:1). When the book of Acts ends, there is a group of believers, part of the universal church, living in Rome (28:24). This extension of the church from east (Jerusalem) to west (Rome) in Acts is a fascinating story. To give it more attention in survey study, one would have to read through Acts another time, watching how the subject of the church is developed chapter by chapter.

* * *

Although the main purpose of a survey of a Bible book is orientation, we should not overlook making

53

personal applications of things we have seen in the book. For instance, a comparison of the beginning and ending of Acts suggests an important spiritual lesson. What Jesus had commissioned and prophesied at the opening of Acts, "Ye shall be witnesses unto me" (1:8) was being accomplished faithfully and unhindered at the end of Acts, "teaching those things which concern the Lord Jesus Christ" (28:31). Now, let us ask ourselves the question, Did the Acts of the Holy Spirit end with the Book of Acts? A thousand times no! There is something about the ending of Acts that suggests an unfinished continuing symphony. The last word in the Greek text is *akōlútos,* meaning "unhindered" (translated in the Authorized Version by four words, "no man forbidding him"). It is as though there is no period at the end of the sentence: Paul would keep on witnessing, and the other Christians would keep on witnessing, and generations after them would keep on witnessing. *And we today should keep on witnessing!*

* * *

You have just read the Book of Acts a few times. Do you suppose that you have learned all there is to learn? Read what John Morley once wrote about this: "It is a great mistake to think that because you have read a masterpiece once or twice or ten times, therefore you have done with it. Because it is a masterpiece you ought to live with it, and make it a part of your daily life." Really, a survey study of a Bible book is only introductory to even more thrilling discoveries in the text.

After you have finished a survey study of a book of the Bible, the next series of studies should be an analysis of each chapter of that book. With the acquaintance you now have of the highlights of Acts,

54

you can see where such a panoramic view of the book will help you in your more detailed study of the smaller parts.[3] In the next chapters we will look at ways to analyze smaller parts of the Bible. In order to afford variety in this book, however, we will go to passages in other books of the Bible, some in the Old Testament, for our examples.

An Exercise for You to Do

You have seen in this chapter how one goes about making a survey study of a Bible book. Acts was the object of such a study.

Why not try surveying another Bible book on your own? This, after all, is your goal: to be able to study the Bible yourself.

Use Exodus as the book for this survey. A minimal set of directions is given below. Record observations on a survey chart whenever possible.

1. Scan the book once or twice for such things as: tone, large movements, turning points, emphases, comparisons and contrasts.

2. Record chapter titles on a survey chart.

3. Contrast the first and last chapters of Exodus. What is the state of Israel in each chapter?

4. Make a list of the major *events* of Exodus and the major *characters*. Record these on the chart.

5. What is the general geographical movement of Exodus?

6. Compare the general content of the first half of Exodus (1-18) with that of the last half (19-40).

7. What is the main difference between the content of chapters 25-31 and that of chapters 35-40?

3. If you are interested in a Bible study manual which will help you continue your analytical studies in Acts, you may want to refer to this author's book, *Acts: An Independent Study* (Chicago: Moody Press, 1968).

8. Name three major truths about God that are prominent in the text of Exodus.

9. Make some outlines for Exodus on such topics as: geography, experiences of Israel, revelation of God.

10. In your own words, what is the theme of Exodus?

11. Try to choose a key verse for Exodus; also identify some key words expressive of the theme of the book.

Chapter 5

Charting a Chapter

CHAPTER STUDY is perhaps the most common of all Bible studies. As earnest Bible students we should always be anxious to learn any methods of study that will help us see more in the biblical text. In this chapter we shall discuss ways to record observations of our study on an analytical chart, hence the title of the chapter, *Charting a Chapter*.

The chapter which we shall study now (Joshua 5) is purposely chosen from the Old Testament to give the reader more confidence in studying in this testament. Much of the Old Testament is overlooked by Christians who wrongly consider it as dry, out of date and too difficult to comprehend. On the contrary—the Old Testament is full of action-packed stories (thrillers if you please), written plainly in the concrete language of the five senses. True, at places there are long lists of genealogy, geography and other necessary citations, but the sincere Bible student will not see these as obstacles in his study. The charge of the Old Testament being out of date is also false—unless God has changed, or sin has taken on a different meaning, or man is no longer a person with intellect, emotions and will.

I. THE CHAPTER AS A STUDY UNIT

When the Bible was first divided into chapter units, practical considerations were probably mostly in mind.

An average chapter's length[1] is a very suitable length for analysis—the time required is reasonable, and the area of focus is workable.

Sometimes a chapter division could have been more favorably located (e.g., chapter 53 of Isaiah should begin with the verse 52:13), but most of the Bible's chapters begin with a new unit of thought. On occasions in chapter study we may choose to identify a passage for analysis to include less than a chapter, or more than a chapter, providing it is still a unit of thought. Such passages could be called segments, since the word "chapter" would not rightly apply. Although the passage we are studying (Joshua 5:2-15) is not a full chapter,[2] we shall nevertheless be referring to it as a chapter, for the sake of simplicity.

II. THE PROCESS OF ANALYSIS

Survey study, which was our exercise in Acts, scans the surface, looking for the big things without tarrying over their details. Analysis study focuses on one part with X-ray eyes, carefully searching even to the hidden chambers of implication and suggestion. The order of all Bible study is this:
1. First, observation (What does the passage say?)
2. Second, interpretation (What does the passage mean?)
3. Third, application (How can this apply to today?)
To observe correctly and fully is to be well on the path to a correct interpretation. This is why observation is so important, and why it will be stressed as we study Joshua 5.

A word might be said here about using outside

1. The average length of a chapter in the Bible is about 26 verses.
2. Verse 1 of Joshua 5 is a natural conclusion to the previous story of the Jordan crossing, begun at 3:1.

helps in Bible study. The key to constructive study habits is to resort to these mainly toward the *end* of our personal study. The temptation comes often to check prematurely what a commentary says about a passage. Discipline yourself to tarry long over just the Bible passage itself, until you have discovered its treasures for yourself. Good outside helps are intended to serve the student as spades, not crutches. The joy of first-hand discovery in Bible study is immeasurable.

III. THE ORIENTATION OF CONTEXT

Before we plunge into the text of Joshua 5, we should see the chapter's setting in the large movement of the book of Joshua. Usually, chapter study is pursued consecutively, with survey of the whole book first (such as we did for Acts in the last chapter), followed by studies in chapter 1, chapter 2, and so forth. When one studies an isolated chapter in the Bible, it is very important to become acquainted with that chapter's context. A Bible commentary is the most practical source of help for this.

The rule of context calls for a consideration of *the whole revelation* of the truth being taught. This applies to both distant context, and immediate context. A familiar illustration of the latter is the story which concerns the battle of Waterloo. All England was waiting to receive the news as to the outcome of the battle. Communication was by semaphore from station to station. One of these was located on top of Winchester cathedral. At a late hour of the day the message was received: "WELLINGTON . . . DEFEATED . . ." Just at that moment a fog descended, and the report of Wellington's disaster was spread throughout London. But when the fog suddenly lifted again, it was seen that there was more to the message. *The full report* was: "WELLINGTON DEFEATED THE

ENEMY." In Bible study we should always consider the whole revelation of the truth being taught.

If you had made a survey study of Joshua, you would have learned that the book is about Israel taking possession of the promised land of Canaan. In Exodus, Israel began its migration from Egypt to Canaan. In Leviticus the nation was given laws to live by, especially for their life in the new land. Numbers narrates their journey through the Sinai wildernesses, and the temporary delay by judgment. Deuteronomy records the preparations made as the people were waiting at the gate to Canaan, opposite Jericho on the plains of Moab, to enter the land under the leadership of Moses' successor, Joshua.

Joshua is the story of *Taking the Inheritance,* an inheritance promised by God. One of its key phrases is, "So Joshua took the whole land" (11:23a).

The story of taking the land inhabited by enemies is told in four parts: Preparation (chapters 1-5); Conquest (chapters 6-12); Inheritances (chapters 13-21); and Consecration (chapters 22-24). The first half of the book (1-12) is filled with ACTION, while the second half records the BUSINESS items of listing the inheritances (13-21), and the appeal of EXHORTATION addressed to the people, as they anticipate dwelling in the new land. These outlines of Joshua are shown on the following chart.

A. The PREPARATION stage (chapters 1-5) involved mobilization and reconnaissance (chapters 1-2); getting into position by crossing the Jordan (3:1-5:1); and spiritual renewal (5:2-15). This last preparation is the object of our present analytical study. When the Israelites fulfilled these spiritual exercises, they were ready to launch out in their campaigns for conquest. Crossing the Jordan (3:1-5:1) brought the nation into geographical position; now they needed to be brought into spiritual position.

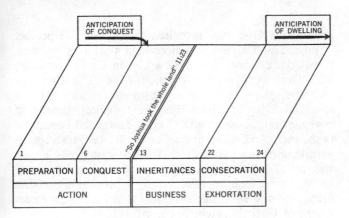

PREPARATION	CONQUEST	INHERITANCES	CONSECRATION
ACTION		BUSINESS	EXHORTATION

B. Joshua's strategy for CONQUEST (chapters 6-12) called for three campaigns: 1) central, involving the key cities of Jericho and Ai (6:1-8:35); 2) southern (9:1-10:43); and 3) northern (11:1-15). The passage 11:16-12:24 is a summary of Joshua's conquests.

C. The business of assigning INHERITANCES (chapters 13-21) called for special allotments (chapters 13-14), and major allotments and special provisions (chapters 15-21).

D. The book ends on the high peak of CONSECRATION (chapters 22-24), centered about the altar of witness (chapter 22) and a renewal of the covenant which God had originally made with Abraham (chapters 23-24).

With this survey of Joshua in mind, we are given a perspective for chapter 5. Note on the chart above where chapter 5 appears. This chapter of spiritual preparation was a vital and necessary exercise for the Israelites, if they were to expect victory in their battles with the enemies. If they did not defeat Satan in their own personal lives and in the life of the nation, they could not expect to drive out the enemies from the land which God had promised them. For the project of possessing Canaan was more than a military venture; it was the entrance into a new life, in God's rest-land, with God as the Lord of their lives. The Book of Hebrews, chapters 3 and 4, interprets for us what this rest-land living involved. For the Israelites already in covenant relationship with God, it demanded continued faith and obedience, and offered all the blessings of partaking of the life of God. The possessing of Canaan was an Old Testament type not of a man becoming saved, but of one, already saved, appropriating all the fulness of the blessings of Christ's Lordship, as "partakers of Christ" (Heb. 3:14; cf. 4:11).

As we study Joshua 5:2-15, therefore, let us look for truths as they bear upon our own Christian life, particularly the victorious life in the fulness of Christ, which is Christian rest-land living.

IV. A Worksheet for Recording Notes

For best results, we should be methodical in recording our studies. Here is a simple worksheet method. Block out a rectangle (about 4″x9″) on a sheet of paper (8½″x11″). For Joshua 5:2-15, block off four paragraphs, beginning at verses 2, 10, 11 and 13. (At the outset of chapter study, we must always identify the paragraphs. We may follow the suggested divisions of our Bible versions, or determine our own set.) Our worksheet should look something like page 63.

Having definite areas on the worksheet encourages orderliness and purpose in our notes. This is an eye-gate aid that will prove invaluable in all our analytical studies.

V. Observations of Joshua 5:2-15

Look . . . look . . . look is a must for fruitful Bible study. This was emphasized in earlier chapters in this book. After we have read this passage a few times, we should begin to record things. Some suggestions, applicable to any segment of study, follow on page 64.

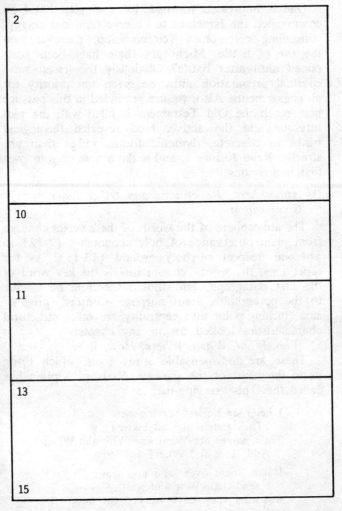

2

10

11

13

15

A. First Impressions

One is impressed to read, for example, that God commanded the Israelites to observe time and energy-consuming ceremonies (circumcision, passover) on the eve of battle. Might not these have been postponed until after battle? Obviously the lesson was: spiritual preparation must be given top priority for all engagements. Also, we are reminded in this passage how much the Old Testament is filled with the picturesque and the active. God revealed theological truths in concrete, dynamic forms, rather than abstractly. Read Joshua 5, and make a note of your own first impressions.

B. Atmosphere, Repetitions and Other Laws of Composition

The atmosphere of the words of these verses changes from plain observance of holy ceremonies (2-12) to awesome respect of holy ground (13-15). As for repetitions, the word "circumcise" is the key word of the first paragraph, and should therefore be a clue to the paragraph's main purpose. Contrast, progression, turning-point and centrality are other structural characteristics looked for in any chapter.

C. Who, What, When, Where, How, Why

These are indispensable study tools, which bring us to the heart of the passage. Rudyard Kipling has called these his "serving-men":

> I keep six honest serving-men
>   (They taught me all I knew);
> Their names are What and Why and When
>   And How and Where and Who
>
> I send them over land and sea,
>   I send them east and west;
> But after they have worked for me,
>   I give them all a rest.

64

Let us apply some of these:

1. *WHAT:* What is the prominent object or action in each paragraph? The answers are clear:

First paragraph (2-9):	circumcision
Second paragraph (10):	passover (blood)
Third paragraph (11-12):	fruit
Fourth paragraph (13-15):	sword

This leads to an associated question: What is each of these a token of?

circumcision	— token of covenant (Cross-reference notes in our Bible or a concordance will direct us to Gen. 17:9-14 for this answer.)
passover blood	— token of atonement (This is shown by Ex. 12:1-20.)
fruit	— token of feasting (not the provisional manna, Ex. 16:15)
sword	— token of victories

In the life of a believer, covenant and atonement have to do with position—LIFE; feasting and victories have to do with experience—LIVING. As we record these on the worksheet, we begin to anticipate some spiritual applications involving Christians:

2. *WHERE:* Let us notice *places* in the passage.

First paragraph:	Egypt, Gilgal
Second paragraph:	plains of Jericho
Third paragraph:	Canaan
Fourth paragraph:	"place . . . holy"

Are any spiritual truths suggested by the places, in view of Israel's past or present experiences? Here are our observations and conclusions:

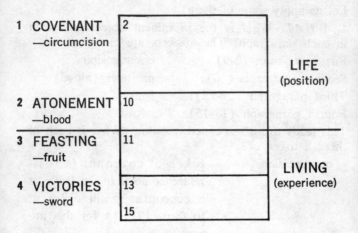

1 COVENANT —circumcision	2	**LIFE** (position)
2 ATONEMENT —blood	10	
3 FEASTING —fruit	11	**LIVING** (experience)
4 VICTORIES —sword	13	
	15	

a. Restoration: Reproach of Egypt (Ex. 32:12) rolled away (Gilgal: literally, "circle").

b. Deliverance assured: In the face of the enemy, on the plains of Jericho.

c. Provision enjoyed: Canaan, a gift of God.

d. Sanctification: The presence of God, in the holy place.

3. *WHO:* Who is the main person of the narrative? God. Let us see how each paragraph shows this.

a. Circumcision: God had initiated the covenant between Himself and Israel (Gen. 17:9-14), and now renews it (Joshua 5:2-9).

b. Passover blood: The key phrase of this rite was always, "When I see the blood, I will pass over you" (Ex. 12:13). The Passover ceremony was originally commanded by God to be an annual event (Ex. 12:14). Up until this time the Israelites had observed it only once (Num. 9:5) since the original event. Now was the time of renewal, to obey God's command again.

66

c. Fruit: The manna ceased at God's bidding, and He gave the new "fruit of the land" (5:12).

d. Sword: God would fight Israel's battles, through His "captain" (5:14).

So the experiences of Israel during this time of spiritual preparation not only reminded them of the prominent place of God in their lives, but also that their God was a gracious *giving* God, showering His gifts on His undeserving people. When we read into the next chapter, this is reiterated at 6:2 concerning the land itself: "See, I have *given* into thine hand Jericho . . . ."

Everything good that we as Christians have is a gift from God. Do we acknowledge this, and thank Him continually?

4. *WHEN:* There is a time reference involving each paragraph.

PAST:

  a. Circumcision — renewing the covenant made earlier with Abraham

  b. Passover — recalling the great Passover deliverance of the exodus

PRESENT and FUTURE:

  c. Fruit—the new diet, advancing from manna to various foods of the field and vine

  d. Sword—assurance of victory in the battles to come

We as Christians look back to our experience of salvation, when we first embarked on the life of the covenant relationship to God, when we were delivered from the bondage of sin by the shed blood of Christ. Having been saved, we now can enter into the fullness of joy which comes as we partake of the wonderful varieties of spiritual food from heaven, and experience

67

the blessings of victories in battle with Satan, by the power of Christ.

5. *HOW and WHY:* These kinds of questions may open doors to the deepest of truths in a passage. For example:

a. How is shed blood acceptable to God for the remission of sins?

b. How did God speak to Joshua and other saints of old?

c. Why did God's captain call that place "holy"?

D. *A Main Outline for the Passage*

We have studied the passage sufficiently now so that we may begin to organize a main outline for the passage. Since this should reflect the main theme of the passage and a key verse, let us state these first:

> *main theme:*
>> For appropriating God's rest-land, there needs to be spiritual renewal of fellowship with God, recognition of His atoning work, a foretaste of blessings to come, and a total dependence on Him for victory.

> *a key verse:*
>> "the land, which the Lord sware . . . that he would give us, a land that floweth with milk and honey" (5:6b).

Now for an outline, based on the theme. There are various ways of wording this. The simpler stated, the better. (See the analytical chart on page 72.)

a main title:	BLESSINGS OF SPIRITUAL REST
	1. Covenant
main paragraph points	2. Atonement
(one per paragraph)	3. Feasting
	4. Victories

If we had worded the title *TOKENS OF SPIRIT-UAL REST,* the tokens themselves would have been the paragraph points: 1) circumcision, 2) blood, 3) fruit, 4) sword.

E. *Subordinate Points in Each Paragraph*

Here we observe the items in each paragraph that support the main point of that paragraph. Let us look for these, and record them on our worksheet. Notice how we derive a spiritual lesson from a historical illustration. Care must be exercised here to avoid extreme spiritualization; nevertheless we need to be alert to the suggestion of historical facts in terms of spiritual application.

BLESSINGS OF SPIRITUAL REST

  I. Covenant (verses 2-9)
  - A. a relationship desired by God (implied in the passage)
  - B. a relationship that demands obedience (verse 6)
  - C. a relationship that dispels reproach (verse 9)

 II. Atonement (verse 10)
  - A. affords a dwellingplace ("encamped")
  - B. gives assurance of sins forgiven ("passover"; "I will pass over you")
  - C. defies the enemy ("in the plains of Jericho")

III. Feasting (verses 11-12)
  - A. bleak survival ceases ("the manna ceased"—verse 12)
  - B. bountiful living begins ("fruit of the land"—verse 12)

 IV. Victories
  - A. the foe is real (verse 13)
  - B. the issue is holy (verse 15)
  - C. the victory is the Lord's (verse 14)

F. *Words and Phrases for Further Study*

For this passage such words might be "passover," "holy," "art thou for us?" Suggestions for word study are given later in this book.

G. *Problem Passages*

If our analysis fails to find answers to problem passages, we should consult a commentary for help.[3] Also we will want to use commentaries as supplementary and checking aids as well, seeking these *after* our independent study.

VI. INTERPRETATIONS AND APPLICATIONS

Interpretations and applications are dependent on observations, but they may be made along the way in one's study, as we have done in this study. Applications should always be made in accord with the spirit and intent of the Bible passage. Interpretation out of context is illustrated by the farmer who went out to the fields to work and encouraged his laziness by recalling Philippians 4:5, "Let your moderation be known unto all men"; then he continued in the folly of his faulty application when he sat down to the dinner table at night with Ecclesiastes 9:10, "Whatsoever thy hand findeth to do, do it with thy might."

The New Testament is of inestimable value for interpreting the Old Testament. Let us look at Hebrews 3 and 4 again, chapters which give the Christian meaning to the Israelites' rest-land living. There we discover some of the blessings of the victorious life. It is interesting to observe how many of these are taught, some by allusion, in the Joshua passage which we have been studying. Included are:

3. A highly recommended one-volume commentary is, Charles F. Pfeiffer and Everett F. Harrison, eds., *The Wycliffe Bible Commentary* (Chicago: Moody Press, 1962).

1. partaking of a heavenly calling (Heb. 3:1)
2. fellowship with Christ, in His house. In fact, we are His house (3:6)
3. partakers of the fullness of Christ (3:14)
4. fruits of faith (4:1-10)
5. the Word of God at work (4:12-13)
6. intercession of Jesus as our High Priest (4:14-15)
7. access to the throne of grace (4:16)
8. help in time of need (4:16)

If these are the blessings, what are the demands on us? From Hebrews the main commands are:

1. hold fast our confidence and profession (3:6; 4:14)
2. believe (3:12) and obey (3:18 "them that believed not" translates a word for "disobedient" ones)
3. come boldly to the throne of grace (4:16)

A Partial List of Key Chapters in the Bible
suggested for analysis

Old Testament	New Testament
Genesis 3	Matthew 5-7
— Fall	— Beatitudes
Genesis 7	Matthew 13
— Flood	— Parables
Genesis 22	Matthew 25
— Sacrifice	— Judgment
Exodus 12	Mark 10
— Passover	— Eternal Life
Exodus 20	Luke 10
— Law	— Service
Exodus 32	Luke 15
— Idolatry	— The Lost
Leviticus 16	John 1
—Sin offering	— Divinity
Leviticus 23	John 3
— Day of Atonement	— Regeneration
Deuteronomy 32	John 6
— Song of Moses	— Bread of Life

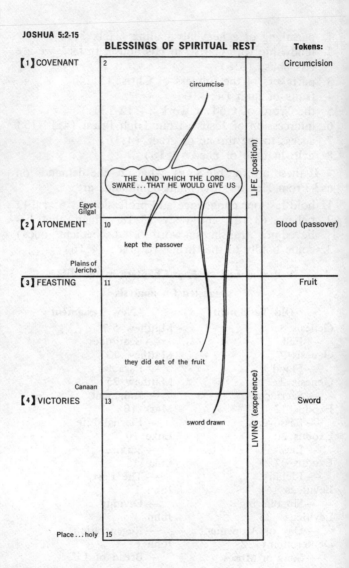

Old Testament	New Testament
Isaiah 52:13-53:12	Colossians 3
— Messiah	— Heavenly Mind
Isaiah 55	I Thessalonians 5
— Universal Call	— Second Coming
Daniel 6	II Timothy 2
— Prayer	— A Good Minister
Hosea 14	Hebrews 1:1-2:4
— Backsliding	— Supreme Revelation
Jonah 2	Hebrews 4
— Deliverance	— Rest
	Hebrews 11
	— Faith
	James 3
	— Tongue
	II Peter 1
	— Abundant Life
	I John 1
	— Walk
	Revelation 2-3
	— Overcomers
	Revelation 22
	— Heaven

An Exercise for You to Do

Analyze Isaiah 6:1-13, recording your observations and outlines on an analytical chart. Make paragraph divisions at verses 1, 5, 8 and 11.

1. Read the chapter once or twice for initial impressions and other observations. As you read try to picture the scene and the action, and try to hear the voices of the speakers. Record paragraph titles.

2. Where in the chapter does Isaiah's call actually begin?

3. What is the main point of each paragraph? Who is the main person of the first paragraph? of the second paragraph? Who asks the question of the third

paragraph, and who asks the question of the fourth paragraph?

4. What is the atmosphere of each of the first two paragraphs?

5. Compare the beginning and end of the chapter.

6. Analyze verses 1-4. Who is the central person, and how is he shown to be central? Study carefully the ascription of verse 3.

7. Analyze verses 5-7. Account for Isaiah's reaction. How does Isaiah identify himself? How does he identify God? What is the purging agent of verses 6-7?

8. Analyze verses 8-10. Observe this outline: Call; Response; Commission. For help in interpreting verses 9-10, read Matt. 13:13-17.

9. Analyze verses 11-13. Observe the two-fold message of judgment and salvation. Note the opening words of verse 13: "But yet."

10. Write out some lessons taught by this chapter about: divine call; Lord's glory; confession of sin; Christian service; hardened hearts; grace of God.

Chapter 6

Probing a Paragraph

THE ORIGINAL WRITERS of the books of the Bible did not divide their books into chapters, paragraphs or verses, because to do so would leave blank spaces on the pages of the manuscript, a prohibitive extravagance in view of the high cost of parchment. In fact in the early writings no empty space was left even between words and sentences. It was up to the reader to re-create the author's writing. Each author followed a plan in writing, even though this did not appear in the format of the manuscripts. He added unit to unit (our chapters), developing each unit by a series of smaller units (our paragraphs). All Bibles published today use a standard set of chapter and verse divisions, but differ as to paragraph divisions.

When a chapter of the Bible is being analyzed, a full analysis of each paragraph must be made, because the paragraphs make the chapter. In chapter 5 we studied the passage Joshua 5:2-15, including its four paragraphs. Since no one paragraph was singled out in that study, it is the purpose of this chapter to focus on one paragraph, and suggest a method of analysis. This is what we call *probing a paragraph*.

The paragraph we shall analyze is I John 1:1-4. It will help to first glance at its context, which includes a little more than the chapter. The study unit is 1:1-2:6. Diagrammed on a worksheet such as we used

76

earlier, the skeleton of this segment might look something like the chart on page 78.

Now let us carefully examine the first paragraph of this segment, verses 1-4. Just as a scientist lays out his specimen on the laboratory table to make a complete, unbiased examination of each part and of the relationships of each part, so we approach this paragraph. A good way to "lay out" the paragraph before us is to print its verses in a box as shown below, a procedure called textual re-creation. The purpose of textual re-creation of this paragraph, with a brief outline in the *margins,* is to *pictorialize* the biblical text showing in visual form not only *what* the text is saying, but *how* it is saying it. Repetitions, comparisons, progressions, are some of the things which we can pictorialize by such writing devices as indentation, underlinings, arrows, and so forth. An example of a simple textual re-creation of this paragraph, with a brief outline placed in the margin, is shown on page 79.

Of course, to make a textual re-creation of a paragraph demands that we *see* things before we *record.* This is the whole point of analysis in scientific examination. We must observe first, record the observations, compare the findings, and reach conclusions.

Remember, in observation we are studying in two areas:

1) what each part says
2) how all the parts are related

Many Bible students stop with the first area, and forfeit all the enlightenment offered by the second area.

Let us observe some of the things that the paragraph I John 1:1-4 is telling us.

A. *Core of a Long Sentence*

In the King James Version the first three verses are one sentence. What is the core of the sentence? That is, what is the main subject, main verb and main

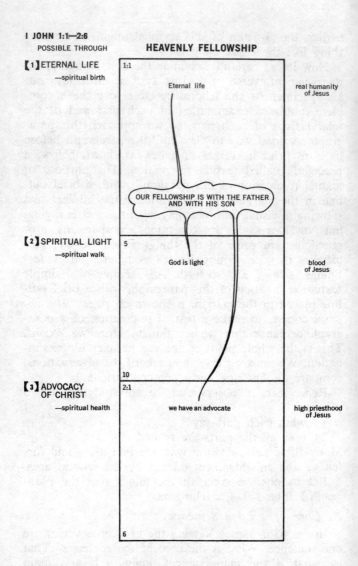

I JOHN 1:1—2:6
POSSIBLE THROUGH

HEAVENLY FELLOWSHIP

【1】ETERNAL LIFE
—spiritual birth

1:1

Eternal life

real humanity
of Jesus

OUR FELLOWSHIP IS WITH THE FATHER
AND WITH HIS SON

【2】SPIRITUAL LIGHT
—spiritual walk

5

God is light

blood
of Jesus

10

【3】ADVOCACY
OF CHRIST
—spiritual health

2:1

we have an advocate

high priesthood
of Jesus

6

TEXTUAL RE-CREATION

WE DECLARE <u>THAT</u>!

I Content of the Message

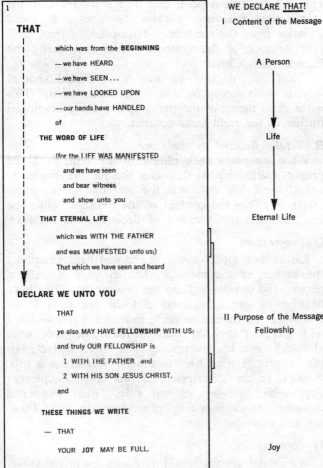

1

THAT

    which was from the **BEGINNING**

    — we have HEARD

    — we have SEEN . . .

    — we have LOOKED UPON

    — our hands have HANDLED

    of

THE WORD OF LIFE

    (for the LIFE WAS MANIFESTED

    and we have seen

    and bear witness

    and show unto you

THAT ETERNAL LIFE

    which was WITH THE FATHER

    and was MANIFESTED unto us;)

    That which we have seen and heard

DECLARE WE UNTO YOU

    THAT

    ye also MAY HAVE **FELLOWSHIP** WITH US:

    and truly OUR FELLOWSHIP is

    1 WITH THE FATHER and

    2 WITH HIS SON JESUS CHRIST.

    and

THESE THINGS WE WRITE

    — THAT

    YOUR **JOY** MAY BE FULL.

4

A Person

Life

Eternal Life

II Purpose of the Message

Fellowship

Joy

object? Main subject: "we." Main verb: "declare." Main object: "that"; indirect object: "unto you." This is John's main point, but he has hidden it in the grammatical structure, because he wanted to focus attention from the start on a description of the "that" (the message of the Gospel), which was really the Person, Jesus Christ.

"That . . . declare we unto you." Stated another way, in exclamatory fashion, "We declare *that*!" This is the main theme of the paragraph, a study developed further in the right-hand column.

B. *Truths Related to the Core*

When we place each phrase of the sentence in its proper relationship to the core, the passage begins to unfold itself. We note that the first half of the paragraph describes the content of the message, while the last half tells the purpose of declaring the message.

C. *Progression*

Let us look more closely at the first half, describing the content of the message. The message is really a person, and obviously, from the descriptions ("we have heard . . . seen . . . handled") the person is Jesus. But He is not named as such; instead He is associated with LIFE. But what kind of life? Life lived unto Himself? Or a life-giving life? The latter; in fact, His life imparts "eternal life" to others. So there is a progression in the description, shown in the sequence: Person $\longrightarrow$ Life $\longrightarrow$ Eternal Life. Other wonderful thoughts are suggested by phrases in the text. These are just some suggestions.

D. *Repetition*

We should always look for repetitions in the Bible. Repetitions are usually easy to detect, and furnish one of the best clues to the intent of a passage. In this paragraph two key repeated words are "life" and "fellowship." But notice another important repetition: two clauses of purposes beginning with the word "that" (meaning "in order that"). John cites two purposes for declaring the gospel of Jesus:

1) "that ye . . . may have fellowship with us" (3)
2) "that your [or our][1] joy may be full" (4)

This is food for thought.

E. *Time References*

When we look for references to "when" in this passage, two explicit ones appear: "beginning" (1) and "eternal" (2). Jesus was not created, but was existing when the creation began. In fact He existed from all eternity past, for He was "with the Father" (2). And He lives into eternity future, for He gives eternal life. What a grand sweeping claim for the Son of God.

F. *Suggested Word Studies*

There are various words and phrases in this passage, suggesting further study. Two of these are "fellowship" and "word of life." Chapter 8 discusses the procedures of word study. We may note here that from the context of this paragraph it may be concluded that only eternally-living persons can have fellowship

1. one with another
2. with the Father
3. with the Son

*   *   *

We have been probing the paragraph I John 1:1-4 to detect its message, especially as this is given by the group of its sentences, or verses. The next logical exercise is to study each particular verse in that paragraph.

1. The question is unsettled as to whether the original text read "our" or "your." The basic application is the same.

Verse study, therefore, is the subject of the next chapter.

An Exercise for You to Do

Analyze carefully this key paragraph of Paul's epistles: Philippians 3:7-14. Print the text phrase by phrase in a paragraph rectangle, showing relations and emphases. Observe how each verse is related to the previous one.

1. Who is the central person of the paragraph? What is taught about him just in this paragraph?

2. Observe repeated words. Make a list of all the strong words of the paragraph.

3. Note how Paul intermingles testimony and aspiration.

4. Observe that all of verses 8-11 is one sentence in the AV. Show by diagram in the textual re-creation of your chart how each phrase is related to the surrounding ones. Observe especially the connecting word "that" (meaning "in order that").

5. Note the positional truth in verse 9, and the experiential truth of the surrounding verses.

6. Study the time references: for example, the past (vv. 7-8); present (8-10); future (11-14).

7. What are the cores of the sentence of verses 13-14? Which is the *major* core?

8. Compare "I count . . . loss" (8) and "I count not . . ." (13).

9. Analyze carefully each small phrase of verse 10. Do the same for verse 14. How is verse 14 a climax of the paragraph?

10. Observe how Paul moves from the "I" of this paragraph to the "we" of the next.

Chapter 7

Examining a Verse

IN THESE CHAPTERS we have moved from the large to
the small in the process of Bible study. We started with
the whole Bible, and saw that though it is a library of
sixty-six books, it is one Book, with one main theme
running throughout its volumes.

Then we surveyed one of the sixty-six books, Dr.
Luke's Acts. We saw how survey of an entire book
is the necessary preliminary step to analysis of its individual chapters.

Next we saw how one studies the Bible chapter by
chapter, which is the heart of Bible analysis. Chapter
study is perhaps the most common exercise in Bible
study, because it is such a workable unit size-wise, and
because it preserves and encourages context study.
The example we used was from Joshua 5.

In the last chapter we focused our eyes on one
paragraph—I John 1:1-4—observing 1) what it said,
and 2) how it said it.

Now, our attention is fixed on just one verse. We
might call this an X-ray examination, for more attention is given here to that which lies beneath the surface of the text.

Verses of course make up paragraphs. The Bible is
filled with verses which are veritable treasure chests
of truth. Most of these are not known by memory.
Then there are the classic verses which have earned

the reputation of being "golden texts" or "key verses." Many of these shine forth in all of their splendor without being remembered for their surrounding context, like Hebrews 4:12. Others are stars in a galaxy of surrounding verses, like Romans 12:1. It is only known in heaven how many single verses in the Bible have been the basis for textual sermons preached since the Scriptures were written.

Let us examine just two verses as examples, noting what variety of truths is revealed in such small compass. Of necessity the analysis made here can only be brief.

> *Romans 1:16* "For I am not ashamed of the gospel of Christ: for it is the power of God unto salvation to every one that believeth; to the Jew first, and also to the Greek."

A. *Grammar*

The core of the sentence is "I (subject) am not ashamed (verb) of the gospel (object)." This is a testimony, suggesting a courageous stand taken by one who might be tempted to be ashamed of the Gospel— the temptation to hold back from preaching it at Rome (1:15) was real, or why was such a testimony worded this way?

The strong verbs of the sentence are: "ashamed" and "believeth." The phrase "not ashamed" seems to suggest one aspect of what is involved in believing.

B. *Type of Content*

There are various types of content in the Bible: history, doctrine, reflection (as in the Psalms), exhortation ("Let us") and command, not to mention such special types as parables and apocalypse (Book of

Revelation). This passage of Romans 1:16 is doctrinal, teaching truths about 1) Gospel of Christ, 2) power of God and 3) salvation of sinners. What is suggested in each?

C. *Facts*

In chapter 5 we saw how Rudyard Kipling's "serving-men" (who, what, when, where, how, why), supplemented by the practical "wherefore," are helpful in Bible study. Miles Coverdale, in the preface to his 1535 English translation of the Bible, talked about these in the following famous lines:

> "It shall greatly helpe ye to understande Scripture,
>   If thou mark
>   Not only what is spoken or wrytten,
>   But of whom,
>   And to whom,
>   With what words,
>   At what time,
>   Where,
>   To what intent,
>   With what circumstances,
>   Considering what goeth before
>   And what followeth."

Let us apply some of these to Romans 1:16:
1. *Persons:* I (Paul), Christ, God, everyone, Jew, Greek.
2. *Subjects:* Gospel (good news) is associated with Christ; power is associated with God; and salvation is associated with people (Jew and Greek).
3. *Time:* a continuing situation is meant by Paul's testimony of allegiance: Paul stood up for the gospel not only on occasion, but continually. Also, a word study on "believeth," with the help of outside sources, would reveal that the believing is a continuous process. There is another time reference in the verse. The phrase

"to the Jew *first*" does not refer to priority of importance, but priority of time. In God's timetable of preaching of the Gospel, the Jews heard it first, then the Greeks, as revealed by Jesus' commission to the disciples, and the witness of the Gospel in Acts.

4. *Place:* the whole world of men: everyone.

5. *What goeth before:* Paul was ready to preach the gospel at Rome (verse 15), because he was not ashamed of that gospel.

6. *What followeth:* Verse 16 states that God can save sinners ("the power of God unto salvation"). Verse 17 tells what salvation really is: receiving the "righteousness of God." This is the answer to the fatal predicament of sin.

D. *Shades of Meaning*

One of the most interesting experiences in Bible study is to compare various versions, to see the full spectrum of shades and colors in the words and phrases of a verse. The necessary economy of words in any one version limits how much the translator can write down as he translates. That is why a comparison of versions, some of which are expanded paraphrases, can be helpful. (See adjacent chart.)

E. *An Outline*

All compound verses lend themselves to some outline. Romans 1:16 might look like this:
    a. A Christian's stand for the Gospel
    b. God's power in the Gospel
    c. Universal audience of the Gospel
Try constructing your own outline.

F. *Words to Study*

Strong words that invite further study are "ashamed," "gospel," "power," "salvation" and "believeth." A word study of "power," for example, would reveal that the

86

King James	Phillips	Living Testament	Today's English Version	New English Bible
"For I am not ashamed	"For I am not ashamed	"For I am not ashamed	"For I have complete confidence	"For I am not ashamed
of the gospel of Christ:	of the Gospel.	of this Good News about Christ.	in the gospel:	of the gospel.
for it is the power of God	I see it as the very power of God	It is God's powerful method	it is God's power	It is the saving
unto salvation	working for the salvation	of bringing to heaven	to save	power of God
to every one	of everyone	all	all	for everyone
that believeth;	who believes it,	who believe it.	who believe,	who has faith—
to the Jew first,	both Jew	This message was preached first to the Jews alone,	first the Jews	the Jew first,
and also to the Greek."	and Greek."	but now everyone is invited to come to God in this same way."	and also the Gentiles."	but the Greek also."

English word in this verse translates the Greek word *dunamos,* from which our word "dynamite" is derived.

* * *

Let us move on to another verse, following the same procedures as above.

> Hebrews 2:3 "How shall we escape, if we neglect so great salvation; which at the first began to be spoken by the Lord, and was confirmed unto us by them that heard him?"

Note: a full analysis of verse 3 should include verses 2 and 4, which complete the thought of the sentence. Because of the limitation of space here, we will discuss only verse 3, but we will keep the context of the two surrounding verses in view. It will become plain, in fact, that verse 3 depends on verse 2 for its accurate interpretation.

A. *Grammar*

This verse is obviously a rhetorical question, asked for effect, not for information. The expected response is, "We shall not, yea, we cannot escape."

The core of the verse is, "We (subject) shall escape (verb) how (object)?"

The strong verbs of the verse are, "escape," "neglect," "spoken," "confirmed" and "heard."

A textual re-creation of the verse reveals its interrelations, and shows the importance of the two small words "how" and "if." (See adjacent chart.)

B. *Type of Content*

This verse is doctrinal and practical, with the impact of warning. The point is, We cannot escape recompense for neglecting so great a salvation as is

"HOW shall we **ESCAPE,**

IF we **NEGLECT** SO GREAT SALVATION

WHICH ◄────

1) at the first began to be

SPOKEN BY THE LORD,

2) and was **CONFIRMED** UNTO US

BY THEM THAT HEARD HIM?"

ours, so let us see to it that we give earnest attention to it! If the "we" refers to Christians, as will be shown below, then this verse is practical teaching concerning Christian living.

C. *Facts*

1. *Persons:* "we"; "the Lord"; "them that heard him." The "we" are believers, as indicated by the context. (Compare such verses as 1:2 ["us"]; 2:1, 9; 3:1 ["our"].) This being the case, Hebrews 2:3 should be applied to Christians, and does not mean, at least in the intent of the setting, "How shall we escape [eternal judgment] if we [reject] so great salvation?"

2. *Subjects:* There are two main subjects in this verse. 1) the inescapable judgments. Every transgression brings recompense (2:2). This applies to everyone, including Christians. 2) neglecting the great salvation. Unbelievers can *reject* what they do not have; Christians can *neglect* what they already have. (On the use of the word "neglect" recall Paul's words to Timothy: "Neglect not the gift that is in thee," I Tim. 4:14.) There are various ways we may neglect our salvation,

89

which the Book of Hebrews speaks about: for example, by not obeying God's Word (2:1); not feeding on the strong meat of the Word (5:11-6:20); not appropriating the privileges of prayer (10:19ff.); not believing (4:1-3).

The unreasonableness and sinfulness of neglecting so great salvation is shown by reminding believers that the very Lord Himself—His message and His life—is being neglected.

3. *Time:* There is a time sequence in the verse:

1) message of salvation spoken by the Lord
2) Lord's message confirmed by first-hand witnesses (and witnesses of signs, wonders, miracles, spiritual gifts—verse 4)
3) neglect of so great salvation
4) inevitable recompense

No one can escape God's appointments of judgment!

4. *What goeth before:* Verse 2 says that in Old Testament days violation of God's Law ("the word spoken by angels") always brought recompense. This is a universal law of returns, which applies to the words of the Lord (verse 3) in New Testament days as well. In fact there is an *a fortiori* argument here. In chapter 1 the writer of Hebrews shows Christ to be infinitely superior to the angels. The point now is, if the angels' words proved steadfast *how much more* (this is the *a fortiori* argument) the words of Christ.

5. *What followeth:* We have already seen that verse 4 is part of the sentence begun in verse 3. From 2:5 on the writer magnifies Jesus the Son and Redeemer, and gives a hundred and one reasons and helps for the Christian *not* to neglect his great salvation.

D. *Shades of Meaning*

King James	Phillips	Living Testament	Berkeley	New English Bible
"How shall we escape,	"how shall we escape	"What makes us think that we can escape	"how shall we escape	"what escape can there be for us
if we neglect	if we refuse to pay proper attention to	if we are indifferent to	in case we neglect	if we ignore
so great salvation; . . .	the salvation that is offered us today?	this great salvation	so great a salvation?	a deliverance so great?
began to be spoken by the Lord,	through the words of the Lord Himself:	announced by the Lord Jesus Himself,	It had its origin when the Lord spoke;	through the lips of the Lord himself;
and was confirmed unto us	it was confirmed for our hearing	and passed on to us	it was confirmed to us	those who heard him confirmed it to us."
by them that heard him;"	by men who had heard him speak."	by those who heard him speak?"	by those who heard it."	

E. *An Outline*

   1. The greatness of the salvation

   2. The Lord's proclamation of the salvation

   3. The truth of the message of salvation

   4. The inescapable recompense for neglecting the salvation

F. *Words to Study*

The key word to study in this passage is "neglect." What does it mean to "neglect" one's salvation? Two other words for study: "escape," "salvation."

*   *   *

The study of single verses in the Bible is a very rewarding experience. Almost always it will lead the student to other paths of inquiry which he had never anticipated.

An Exercise for You to Do

The most widely memorized verse in the Bible is perhaps John 3:16. Because of its familiarity it is often overlooked as to close scrutiny and analysis. See what you can do with a thorough analysis of this great verse.

1. Examine the verse's neighbors—that is, verses 14-15 and 17. Keep this context in mind.

2. Analyze the grammar of the verse. For example, what is the core?

3. Look for the who, what, where, when, how and why.

4. What would you choose to be the key word or phrase of the verse?

5. Compare the beginning and end of the verse.

6. Are there any contrasts in the verse?

7. What do you see here of cause and effect?

8. What words are picture words? What words are theological?

9. Construct an outline for the verse.
10. What truths, if any, are implied?
11. What words of this verse call for special word study?
12. Compare the reading of the verse in a few modern versions.

The variety of approaches in Bible study keeps one from falling into any routine of sameness, lameness and tameness. Let it be part of your own study habits to analyze single verses in the Bible from time to time. Enjoy verse study!

Below is a recommended list of verses for study. Some of these you may have already memorized, but have you ever analyzed them?

A Selected List of Sixty-Six Golden Verses in the Bible[1]
(one from each book of the Bible)

Genesis 3:15. First Messianic promise.
Exodus 12:13. Life insurance.
Leviticus 25:10. The Year of Jubilee.
Numbers 9:17. The pilgrim's guide.
Deuteronomy 29:29. The secret things.
Joshua 1:8. The price of success.
Judges 16:20. The lost power.
Ruth 1:16. A shining example of constancy.
I Samuel 15:22. The indispensable virtue.
II Samuel 18:33. The father's lament.
I Kings 3:9. The prayer for wisdom.
II Kings 6:17. The divine reinforcements.
I Chronicles 4:10. A wonderful prayer in dark surroundings.
II Chronicles 16:9. The all-seeing eye.
Ezra 7:10. The faithful scribe.
Nehemiah 4:17. A true labor union.
Esther 4:14. The woman for an emergency.
Job 42:10. An enriching prayer.

[1] From *The New Chain-Reference Bible* (Indianapolis: B. B. Kirkbride Bible Co.). Used by permission.

93

Psalm 84:11. The matchless Giver.
Proverbs 3:15. The precious possession.
Ecclesiastes 12:13. The great conclusion.
Song of Solomon 1:6. The unfaithful vineyard keeper.
Isaiah 9:6. The most wonderful child.
Jeremiah 29:13. The greatest discovery.
Lamentations 3:22. God's unfailing mercies.
Ezekiel 33:32. The sentimental hearers.
Daniel 6:10. The unchangeable habit of prayer.
Hosea 6:3. The road to divine blessing.
Joel 2:28. The outpouring of the Spirit.
Amos 8:11. The spiritual famine.
Obadiah 4. The humbling of the proud.
Jonah 1:3. An expensive journey.
Micah 6:8. Practical religion.
Nahum 2:4. Nothing new under the sun.
Habakkuk 2:14. World-wide missions.
Zephaniah 2:3. Seeking the Lord.
Haggai 2:4. A ringing call to duty.
Zechariah 4:6. The true means of success.
Malachi 3:10. The tither's promise.
Matthew 7:7. The three-fold promise.
Mark 16:15. The great commission.
Luke 10:20. The real reason for joy.
John 15:7. The master-key of prayer.
Acts 1:8. The watchword of the spiritual campaign.
Romans 10:9. The plan of salvation.
I Corinthians 3:11. The only foundation.
II Corinthians 4:6. The illuminated heart.
Galatians 2:20. Dying to live.
Ephesians 4:13. The highest development.
Philippians 2:5. The mind of Christ.
Colossians 3:1. The heavenly ambition.
I Thessalonians 5:23. Entire sanctification.
II Thessalonians 3:10. The duty to labor.
I Timothy 4:12. The young man's example.
II Timothy 2:4. The soldier's separation.
Titus 2:14. The Redeemer's purpose.
Philemon 15. A tender appeal.

Hebrews 11:13. The pilgrims' vision.
James 5:20. The soul-winner's achievement.
I Peter 1:18, 19. The cost of redemption.
II Peter 1:21. The origin of prophecy.
I John 3:2. The sons of God.
II John 6. Love and obedience.
III John 4. The minister's joy.
Jude 24, 25. The divine keeper.
Revelation 11:15. The consummation of the divine plan.

Chapter 8

Weighing a Word

THE STUDY of single Bible words, weighing them to determine their content and function, can be one of the most fascinating exercises of the Christian. Wilbur M. Smith writes, "There is no book in the world whose words will yield such treasures of truth, such spiritual richness, such rivers of refreshing water, such strengthening of the soul as the words with which the Holy Spirit has inspired the authors of the books of our Bible."[1]

When we think how many different words there are in the Bible,[2] we might wonder what weight one word can have among so many. But then we are reminded that "it is the aggregation of the littles that makes the whole."[3] Just as a great door swings on small hinges, the important theological statements of the Bible often depend upon even the smallest words, such as prepositions and articles. Using another picture, one writer has said that as the smallest dewdrop on the meadow

1. *Op. cit.,* p. 43.
2. The Hebrew Old Testament contains 6,413 different words, exclusive of proper names, which represent about 1,860 Hebrew roots. The Greek New Testament contains 4,867 different words. In the English Bible there are a total of about 6,000 different words.
3. Arthur T. Pierson, *Knowing the Scriptures* (New York: Gospel Publishing House, 1910), p. 117.

at night has a star sleeping in its bosom, so the most insignificant passage of Scripture has in it a shining truth.

Hebrew and Greek scholars inform us what rich language is to be found in the testaments of those original languages. Robert B. Girdlestone says this about the Hebrew language: "Its definite article . . . its mode of marking emphasis and comparison, the gravity and solemnity of its structure, the massive dignity of its style, the picturesqueness of its idiom— these make it peculiarly fitting for the expression of sacred truth."[4] Richard C. Trench speaks as enthusiastically for the Greek language, which he describes as one "spoken by a people of the subtlest intellect, who saw distinctions, where others saw none; who divided out to different words what others often were content to huddle confusedly under a common term; who were themselves singularly alive to its value, diligently cultivating the art of synonymous distinction . . .; and who have bequeathed a multitude of fine and delicate observations on the right discrimination of their own words to the afterworld."[5]

But how does this pertain to the majority of Bible students who are not acquainted with the Hebrew or Greek, and who might very well say, "It's *all* Greek to me!"? Has the beauty and depth and fullness of those original languages been carried over into the English, our mother tongue? This aspect of translation — equivalent carry-over even as to the color and shades of words—has always been a great challenge to Bible

4. Robert B. Girdlestone, *Old Testament Synonyms* (Grand Rapids: Wm. B. Eerdmans Publishing Co., reprint edition, 1953), pp. 6-7.

5. Richard C. Trench, *Synonyms of the New Testament* (Grand Rapids: Wm. B. Eerdmans Publishing Co., reprint edition, 1948), p. vii.

translators. In chapter 1 of this book we pointed out that the Bible is a miracle book even as to the translation process, God giving special gifts of wisdom to the men entrusted with this important task. The King James translators, relying heavily upon the earlier work of William Tyndale and John Wycliffe, surely succeeded in matching the excellence of the Hebrew and Greek versions which they were translating, as evaluated thus by one writer:

> But always in considering this, our English classic [King James Version], we must remember that behind it were the world's profoundest religious truths uttered by Hebrews in concrete, vivid, figurative expression. It was this rich ore which was cast into the English crucible to be heated hot with religious fervor and with the zest of a new intellectual awakening . . . . Out of the fire came this book, so simple, direct and suggestive in language, so beautiful and resonant in rhythm, so majestic and inspiring in tone that as literature it is said even to surpass the original, and no one influence has been so great in the life of English-speaking people, religiously, morally, socially, politically, as has this version.[6]

It encourages us in Bible study to know that the words which God inspired in the original languages have not been watered down in the translation processes over the centuries.

The only place where God has chosen to record the full revelation of eternal life is in the Bible, a book wrapped in the "swaddling-clothes" of human words. If we are to know the *Word,* we must study the *words.*

6. Laura H. Wilk, *The Romance of the English Bible* (New York: Doubleday, Doran and Co., 1929), pp. 195-96.

Let us now look at ways to learn the full meaning of a Bible word.

I. Two Approaches of Word Study

There are basically two approaches to the study of a Bible word: context approach, and comparative approach.

A. *Context Approach*

Here we study a word to learn its contribution and function in the context of an isolated verse, paragraph or chapter. Examples of this approach were given in the earlier chapters when we studied the above-named units. In this kind of study, the following inquiries will yield some very interesting answers. Let us suppose we are studying the word "faith" as it appears ten times in the fourth chapter of Romans.

1. What would we know about faith if this chapter were the entire Scriptures?

2. Could any other word have served the same purposes in these ten references?

3. How much does the chapter contribute to the meaning of the word "faith"; and how much does the word "faith" contribute to the meaning of the chapter? Let us look a little bit more closely at the former of these: how much does the chapter contribute to the meaning of the word "faith"? A concordance reveals that the *word* "faith" appears ten times in the chapter, but on reading the chapter it is clear that the *concept* of "faith" is described and illustrated in various ways. For example, look at Abraham's faith, and see the various shades and qualities of that faith as they are progressively recorded in verses 17-21:

    1) He considered *hopeful* what appeared *hopeless;* "who against hope believed in hope" (v. 18)

    2) He accepted as *possible* what appeared *impos-*

sible; "being not weak in faith, he considered not his own body now dead" (v. 19)

3) He did not waver or hesitate over the great promise of God; "he staggered not at the promise of God" (v. 20)

4) He placed full assurance in the omnipotence of God "being fully persuaded that, what he (God) had promised, he was able also to perform" (v. 21)

Each of the above four references presents a different *shade* of what real faith is.

B. *Comparative Approach*

This method of studying a word, a restricted form of topical study, observes how a particular word is used throughout the entire Bible. The remainder of this chapter is about this comparative method.

There are three main rules for weighing a Bible word, to learn its total contribution to the Scriptures. Let us look at each of these, applying them to the Bible word "fulness."

II. RULES FOR WEIGHING A WORD

A. *Check its occurrences in the Bible.*

For this, we need the help of an exhaustive concordance. Strong's *Exhaustive Concordance*[7] and Young's *Analytical Concordance*[8] are the standard works. References below are to the former.

Some strong words of the Bible appear so often that it may not be possible, in a study exercise limited by time, to refer to every verse cited by the concordance

---

7. *Op. cit.* Strong's concordance is for quicker reference of the *English* words; Young's concordance is organized more with reference to the Hebrew or Greek words translated by the English words.

8. Robert Young, *Analytical Concordance to the Bible* (Grand Rapids: Wm. B. Eerdmans Publishing Company).

(e.g., the word "heaven"). In such cases, by reading the phrases in the concordance we are usually able to select those verses which we will want to read in their entirety. The word "fulness" does not appear that often, and so we would be able to easily read all the references.

When we first locate the word "fulness" in the concordance, these are our preliminary observations:

1. number of occurrences: 25
2. distribution as to testament: about equally divided
3. books where the word appears more frequently: Psalms (6 times) and Ephesians (4 times)
4. any particular pattern of appearance: It is interesting to note that except for the one reference in John, Paul is the only New Testament writer to use the word.

B. *Find the root meaning.*

Now we get to the heart of our study, which is, what does the word mean? An English dictionary will help define the English word, but why not search for the word's meaning in the original languages, if this is possible? The directions below show how the average student of the English Bible can make a non-technical study of the root meanings of the Hebrew and Greek words.

There are various outside helps for this kind of study.[9] The average Bible student can learn much, however, from his exhaustive concordance regarding this. For example, Strong's concordance gives a number opposite each reference, each number representing the Hebrew or Greek word which the English word translates. The Old Testament references of course refer to Hebrew words (listed by number in the back

9. For example, Bible dictionaries and encyclopedias, and special studies (e.g., Girdlestone's and Trench's books on synonyms, cited earlier).

of the concordance under *Hebrew and Chaldee Dictionary*); the New Testament references refer to Greek words (listed by number under *Greek Dictionary of the New Testament*). Similar numbers (e.g., 4393 and 4395) usually refer to the same roots.

O.T. references for "fulness"

	#4395—Num. 18:27
group	#4393—Deut. 33:16; I Chr. 16:32; Ps. 24:1;
1	50:12; 89:11; 96:11; 98:7; Ezek. 19:7
	#4390—Job 20:22
group	#7648—Ps. 16:11
2	#7653—Ezek. 16:49

N.T. references for "fulness"

	#4138—(all the N.T. references use this one
only	Greek word): John 1:16; Rom. 11:
one	12, 25; 15:29; I Cor. 10:26, 28;
group	Gal. 4:4; Eph. 1:10, 23; 3:19; 4:13;
	Col. 1:19; 2:9

When we consult the Hebrew and Greek dictionaries at the back of the concordance, here are our findings:

Hebrew

#4390. The root is *mawlaw,* meaning "to fill or be full of," in a wide application, etc. We read Job 20:22 in the light of this: "In the FULNESS of his [the wicked man's] sufficiency he shall be in straits . . . ."

#4393. *Melo,* from #4390. "All that is therein." When we read the verses using this form of the word, we find they are all similar. For example: "The earth is the Lord's, and the FULNESS thereof . . ." (Ps. 24:1).

#4395. Traced back to the root of #4390, *mawlaw.* "Something fulfilled," that is, "abundance of produce." The one verse using this form is

102

Num. 18:27, with its reference to "the FUL-NESS of the winepress."

Now we turn to the second group of numbers, 7648 and 7653, which suggests a different root from the one we have been noting.

#7648. We are directed by the concordance to the number 7646, which shows the root *sawbah,* meaning "to fill to satisfaction." The key word here is *satisfaction.*

#7653. The same root, *sawbah.*

Our curiosity is aroused to read the two verses using this *different* word "fulness":

"Thou wilt show me the path of life:
In thy presence is FULNESS of joy,
At thy right hand there are pleasures for evermore" (Ps. 16:11).
"Behold, this was the iniquity of thy sister Sodom, pride, FULNESS of bread, and abundance of idleness was in her . . . " (Ezek. 16:49).

Our tentative conclusion is that "fulness" of this second group *(sawbah)* has a different connotation from the "fulness" of the first group *(mawlaw). Mawlaw* connotes full scope; *sawbah* connotes full satisfaction.

Now let us look at the New Testament references:

Greek

#4138. The word is *pleroma,* traced back to the root *pimplemi* (#4130): "fill, fulfill, accomplish, furnish."

The observation we make here is that this Greek root has the same connotation as the Hebrew *mawlaw* (fulness as to scope), not the root *sawbah* (fulness as to satisfaction).

With the above root meanings in mind, we read the various New Testament verses, where

103

the Old Testament picture of *mawlaw,* a full unit—with no voids—is applied to theological truths, e.g., "and of his FULNESS have all we received, and grace for grace." All of the verses seem to use the word "fulness" in the same way with the possible exception of Rom. 15:29, where the idea of satisfaction *appears* to be meant, because of the word "blessing" in the context. A further study will clarify this.

C. *Recognize its usage.*

The *root* meaning of a word sheds light on the word's origin, but in the final analysis the *usage* of the word is the primary determinant of its meaning.

1. *Usage in extra-biblical literature.* Except for an exhaustive study of the word by the advanced student, this step of investigation is not a necessary one. For those interested in pursuing it, special works (e.g., *The Vocabulary of the Greek Testament,* by James H. Moulton and George Milligan)[10] would have to be consulted. Here we learn, for example, how people on the street used the Greek word *pimplemi* outside of any religious context. A fourth century manuscript has this phrase: "Fill *(pimplemi)* the vessel with green mustard."[11] This shows that the New Testament writers used the word in the same way the word was used in everyday life. We are told that the word *pleroma* probably was not used often in the vernacular. One manuscript, dated 240 B.C., writes, "You wrote me not to withdraw the gang *(pleroma)* from Philoteris before they had finished the work." The word thus used means "full company" or "complement."

2. *Usage in the Bible.* How a word is used in the Bible indicates the precise meaning of that word, *as*

10. London: Hodder and Stoughton, Limited, 1952.
11. *Op. cit.,* p. 513.

a Bible word. One can see here why context study is so vital in this respect.

a. first usage in the Bible. It is always interesting to see how certain words were used in their first biblical appearance. For example, note how the word "knowledge" was used in Gen. 2:9. We must be careful, however, not to foster a law of interpretation here which would require that the first usage of a word in the Bible must determine the meaning of the word in all subsequent appearances.

b. most frequent usage in the Bible. We have seen that the word "fulness" is used in two different ways in the Bible: 1) full scope and 2) total satisfaction. The former is the most common; the latter appears only in two of the 25 occurrences.

c. comparison of Old and New Testament usages:
   Old Testament: word is used both ways
   New Testament: word is used just with the thought of full scope

d. areas of application. Let us briefly look at the word "fulness" as it appears in its most common form, that of full scope (Hebrew *mawlaw* and Greek *pleroma*). Here we want to note the various areas of its application. By comparing the verses and collating them, the following outline emerges, rather naturally:

I. THE MATERIAL WORLD
   A. *Fulness of Nature*
      1. earth (Deut. 33:16; Ps. 24:1; I Cor. 10:26, 28)
      2. land (Ezek. 19:7)
      3. world (Ps. 50:12; 89:11)
      4. sea (I Chr. 16:32; Ps. 96:11; 98:7)
      5. winepress (Num. 18:27)

105

B. *Fulness of Things*
   —possessions (Job 20:22). (The interesting
   lesson to learn here is that wealth does not
   help the real plight of the wicked man:
   "he shall be in straits.")

II. THE SPIRITUAL WORLD
   A. *Fulness of the Trinity*
      1. God (Eph. 3:19)
      2. Godhead (Col. 1:19; 2:9)
      3. Christ (John 1:16; Eph. 4:13)
   B. *Fulness of the Message of God*
      —the Gospel's blessing (Rom. 15:29)
   C. *Fulness of the Family of God*
      1. Israel (Rom. 11:12)
      2. Church (Eph. 1:23)
   D. *Fulness of the Calendar of God*
      1. the time (Gal. 4:4)
      2. times (Eph. 1:10)
      3. Gentiles (Rom. 11:25)

The above outline should suggest many blessed
truths to the Christian. For example, the fulness of
the blessing of Christ's gospel (Rom. 15:29) is for
us today. How big is it? Can one even measure it?
We may not comprehend such total blessing, but taking the phrase "FULNESS of the earth" (Ps. 24:1)
as a quantitative measuring stick we are overwhelmed
by Paul's reference to the bigness of the Gospel's
blessing.

Consider "the FULNESS of God" (Eph. 3:19). We
can easily accept such a theological phrase, for is not
God the Cause of all things, creating and upholding
His universe? But it is difficult to believe that we can
be filled with this fulness of God. And yet Paul was
inspired of the Spirit to record this very practical,

106

glorious truth, that a Christian can be "filled with all the FULNESS of God."

Do we have goals for our Christian journey? Have we ever considered the goal of the "FULNESS of Christ" (Eph. 4:13)? That was the goal Paul was interested in: "till we all come . . . unto a perfect man, unto the measure of the stature of the FULNESS of Christ." There surely is no higher goal in life.

Such are the kinds of thoughts that come to the Bible student when studying a Bible word. Should we not engage more often in this enjoyable and profitable kind of study?

A Selected List of Key Bible Words for Comparative Study

access	holy	reconcile
atone	Immanuel	redeem
baptize	iniquity	repent
believe	Jehovah	rest
bless	Jesus	righteous
chasten	kingdom	sabbath
Christ	know	sacrifice
church	law	saint
covenant	life	save
death	Lord	sin
disciple	love	spirit
evil	manifest	temptation
faint	mercy	truth
favor	minister	understand
fellowship	name	vain
good	obey	vision
gospel	passover	watch
grace	peace	wisdom
hear	perfect	word
hell	preach	

An Exercise for You to Do

A key word in the Bible is the word "love." A quick glance at a concordance reveals how often it appears in both testaments.

Make a study of the word as it appears in the New Testament. Observe from the concordance that there are two main New Testament words for love: one which translates *agapaō* (#25 in Strong's concordance); and one which translates *phileō* (#5368). Study John 21:15-17 for an interesting juxtaposition of the two Greek words. Continue your comparative study by observing how the words are used in other verses, separately.

Concentrate your study, however, on the word which translates *agapaō*. Arrive at a full definition of the word. (Note: a topical study of "love" will be made at the end of chapter 9.)

Chapter 9

Organizing a Topic

TOPICAL BIBLE STUDY is a custom-made type of study, usually arising out of a situation or need. For instance, as we read about the Arab-Israel relations in the newspapers, we would like to know what the Bible says about the Jew. And so we would make a topical study about *The Jew*—just what the *Bible* has to say about this subject. Ecumenical stirrings suggest a study about the Church; the tongues movement, a study about gifts of the Spirit; the "new" morality, a study about sin and the Law of God; and wars between nations, a study about war. Topical sermons delivered from the pulpits of our churches are based on such topical studies in the Bible.

Topical study goes one step further than word study. Whereas word study stays within the boundaries of analyzing the meaning of the particular word itself, topical study moves freely about a general subject, studying synonyms, antonyms and even references that are only implied in passages. It is obvious why a concordance is limited in this respect.

Outside helps are very desirable for topical study. *Nave's Topical Bible*[1] was compiled particularly to serve this kind of study. Chain-reference notes in Bibles are helpful.[2] For the study of doctrines, books

1. Chicago: Moody Press.
2. E.g., the Thompson chain-reference Bible cited earlier.

on theology are very helpful. Then there are volumes on individual subjects, like Herbert Lockyer's *All the Prayers of the Bible*.[3]

I. PROCEDURE OF TOPICAL STUDY

The procedure of topical study is simple, following a natural inductive approach of beginning with unrelated facts and bringing them together to an organized whole. Involved are three exercises, described below.

A. *Build a list of Bible references whose passages contribute something to the subject.*

At this point we are not so concerned with reading the passages themselves, as we are in finding the references. To find such, we start with a concordance, then move on to other source books, such as those mentioned above (Nave's Topical Bible, books on doctrine, Bible dictionary, and so forth). The references are listed in one column, on the left-hand side of the paper, leaving room for later notations.

Suppose we wanted to study the subject of *angels,* with special reference to good angels. Some of the verses which we would come up with, from the above sources, would include: Gen. 3:24; 6:2, 4; 19:11-13; Deut. 18:10-12; I Sam. 4:4; II Sam. 14:20; II Kings 19:15; Neh. 9:6; Job. 1:6; 2:1; 33:23; 38:4-7; Ps. 18:9-10; 68:17; 80:1; 91:11; 99:1; 103:20; 104:4; 148:2,5; Isa. 6:1-2, 6; 8:19-20; Ezek. 9:1, 5, 7; 10:1-20; 28:14-16; Dan. 3:28; 6:22; 7:10, 16; 9:21; 10:13, 21; 12:1; Matt. 1:20; 4:11; 13:39, 49-50; 16:27; 18:10; 22:30; 24:36; 26:53; 28:2-7; Luke 1:26-38; 2:8-15; 4:34; 16:22; 20:34-36; 22:43; John 1:51; Acts 1:11; 5:19; 12:7, 11, 23; I Cor. 6:3; 10:20-21; Eph. 1:21; 6:12; Col. 1:16; 2:18; I Thess. 4:16-18; II Thess. 1:7; I Tim. 4:1; 5:21; 6:16; Heb. 1:6-7, 14; 2:16; 12:22-23; 13:2; I Pet. 1:12; II Pet.

3. Grand Rapids: Zondervan Publishing House.

2:11; Jude 9; Rev. 5:11; 9:20-21; 12:7-12; 14:6; 21:1-2, 12.

B. *Read the various passages.*

As we read, we jot down on paper opposite each reference the main truths taught about angels by each verse. Brief notations are recommended, to help in our next step of organization.

C. *Organize the individual facts under topical headings.*

To do this, we must first read over the brief notations we have already recorded for each verse, correlating passages of similar teaching. Eventually, in this step of synthesizing, each verse will fall under one group of common content. Then the groups will suggest an outline. For the subject of angels, such an outline might look like this:

I. ORIGIN OF ANGELS
   A. Creation
   B. Time of their creation
   C. Number

II. NATURE OF ANGELS
   A. Not glorified human beings
   B. Incorporeal
   C. A company; not a race
   D. Powers

III. MINISTRY OF GOOD ANGELS
   A. Past ministry
   B. Present ministry
   C. Future ministry

II. TWO KINDS OF TOPICAL STUDY

There are two different kinds of topical study: broad and explicit. Listed below are examples of each of these.

A. *Broad Subjects*
  1. characters of the Bible (e.g., such groups as patriarchs, martyrs, kings, women, disciples)
  2. crises of the Bible
  3. key doctrines of the Bible
  4. prayers of the Bible
  5. conversions of the Bible
  6. sermons of the Bible
  7. calls to service
  8. surnames of the Bible
  9. the Scriptures
  10. revivals in the Bible

B. *Explicit Subjects*
  1. names of God
  2. titles of Christ
  3. crises of Christ's life
  4. parables of Jesus
  5. invitations of Jesus
  6. 10 great sermons of Acts (5 by Peter; 1 by Stephen; 4 by Paul)
  7. Paul the missionary
  8. the 6 "precious" things of Peter's epistles
  9. the 7 "blesseds" and 8 "overcomeths" of Revelation
  10. the "better" things of Hebrews
  11. the "I am's" of John
  12. the "fear of the Lord" of Proverbs
  13. the 7 "forty days" of the Bible

Perhaps the most interesting and enlightening kind of topical study is the study of a Bible character. Almost 3,000 men and women appear by name in the text of the Bible. Not a little biographical data is given for many of these. This does not surprise us, for biblical truth is clothed with the garment of facts, the most important of which are the *experiences of people*. The Bible speaks to our *lives;* hence the important place given in it to the lives of people. We are mainly *onlookers* when we read about historical events; we are intimate *participators* when we read biography or autobiography.

A Bible dictionary usually supplies the main biblical references pertaining to any one Bible character.

Whenever we study the life of a person in the Bible, we should look for the following:

1. name(s); surname; and significance of each
2. ancestry. What does the Bible say of the parents?
3. environment; training
4. desirable and undesirable traits
5. friendships
6. conversion; other crises
7. influence by others and upon others
8. spiritual growth
9. work accomplished
10. sins and shortcomings
11. Bible's evaluation of the person
12. years lived
13. lessons to be learned from this person's life

* * *

Our minds can hardly conceive of a subject that is not treated in the Bible. Even such modern subjects as space, psychology, teaching methods, riots, authority, law and taxes appear throughout the Book. Bible encyclopedias and dictionaries attest to the vast scope of subject matter in the Bible. This is noteworthy in view of the fact that the Bible does not pretend to be a textbook in such areas as the arts and sciences. John Greenleaf Whittier gave expression to this in the familiar lines:

We search the world for truth. We cull
The good, the pure, the beautiful
From graven stone and written scroll,
And all old flower-fields of the soul;
And, weary seekers of the best,
We come back laden from our quest,
To find that all sages said
Is in the Book our mothers read.

Nothing recorded in the Bible is superfluous. That which has been recorded contributes in some way to the grand theme of God's Offer of Salvation to Mankind by Jesus Christ. The many kinds of extensive topical studies that may be derived from the Scriptures suggest how vast that grand theme really is.

Two Exercises for You to Do

1. Barnabas is an interesting New Testament character, from whose life some important spiritual lessons may be learned. Study every New Testament verse, with its context, which makes reference to this man. See how many things you can learn about him, and make a list of the practical lessons being taught.
2. For another topical study, continue the word study of "love" begun in the previous chapter. For this project, observe the various aspects of *agape* in the New Testament, and arrive at an outline of the topic. Such an outline might include such subjects as 1) divine love, 2) walk of Christian love, 3) fruits of love. Choose from a concordance the verses you want to use in your study. For an abridged study of the word, identify what each of the following verses teaches about love:

I John 4:8-10, 16	I Cor. 16:22	John 13:35
I Cor. 13:4-7, 13	Rom. 5:8	I Thess. 4:9
Matt. 22:37-40	John 16:27	Titus 2:4
Rom. 13:8-10	Heb. 12:6-11	Matt. 5:43-48

John 17:23-24
John 3:16
Gal. 2:20
Eph. 2:4-5

Rom. 8:31-39
Rom. 5:5
II Cor. 5:14-15
Gal. 5:13

Rom. 12:9
I John 3:18
Col. 3:14

APPLYING THE BIBLE

Chapter 10

Putting the Bible to Work

IN THE PREVIOUS CHAPTERS we have seen that enjoyment of the Bible comes to the Christian for a full appreciation, sound approach, personal absorption and careful analysis of its pages. As we have tarried over each of these, the point has been made that our ultimate goal in Bible study is not to do something to the Book, but to let it do something to us. *Observation* and *interpretation* are not enough. It is *application* which completes the Bible study process. When a young Chinese student was asked how he was getting along in his Bible study, he replied, "I am now reading the Bible and behaving it."

Let us reiterate this important aspect of *applying* the Word, as we come to the end of our discussion of enjoying this Book of God. We shall use simple diagrams to illustrate the point.

This circle represents the Bible, which is the Word of God.

WORD
OF
GOD

What a mighty Word it is! Its potential is beyond all comprehension. Its message, the gospel, is dynamite (Rom. 1:16). God would have this Word to be at the center of our lives—instructing, motivating, empowering us. So let us put this circle in the center of a larger circle, which represents our lives, thus:

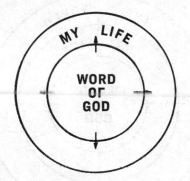

The arrows represent the ever-active work of the Word. In its work of diagnosis, the Word exposes the cancer of sin and brings conviction (Heb. 4:12-13). In its healing work it cleans and purifies (John 15:3; 17:17; Eph. 5:25-26). Its manna gives strength for living (Deut. 8:3), and its sword equips for battle (Eph. 6:17). As a manual it gives counsel for our walk (Ps. 119:24), and as waters flowing from the throne of God it brings forth fruit to the glory of God (Ps. 1:2-3). There is no book in all the world like this! The writer Izaak Walton (1593-1683) penned four short lines to tell what the Bible meant in his life:

> Every hour
> I read you, kills a sin,
> Or lets a virtue in
> To fight against it.

But there is a larger ministry of the Word. This ministry, launched in the Great Commission (Matt. 28:19-20), affects the whole, wide world. So let us put the circle of the Word, and of My Life, in the center of the circle of The World:

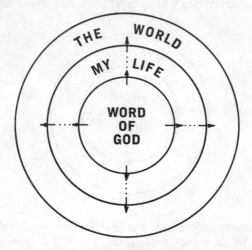

Again, the arrows represent the activity of the Word: the Word not merely working *in* my life, but also working in the world *through* my life. This is God's full design for putting the Bible to work.

Now let us get a little more specific in our discussion of personal application of the Bible. Both the Old and New Testaments were written with two basic purposes: to point unbelievers to the *way to God,* and to show believers how to *walk with God.* Paul made this very clear when he wrote his last inspired letter to Timothy, reminding his friend and co-laborer that the holy Scriptures which Timothy had learned from childhood (at that time the Scriptures included only the Old Testament) were able to make him "wise unto salvation" (II Tim. 3:15). This was teaching concerning the *way to God*. Also, Paul wrote, all Scripture was given by God "so that the man who serves God may be fully qualified and equipped to do every kind of good work" (II Tim. 3:17, *Today's English Version*). Paul was telling Timothy that the Scriptures were to equip him to walk acceptably with his God. This was teaching concerning *walk with God*. It is correct to say that all spiritual lessons derived from passages in the Bible have something to say, directly or indirectly, about these two vital life-truths: *way* to God, or *walk* with God.

Personal application of the Bible becomes an easier task and a more natural habit when we are convinced that the Bible offers up-to-date instruction, that it concerns us personally, and that its spiritual lessons are not hazy or ambiguous. This suggests some important rules for applying the Scriptures to everyday life.

1. *Expect the Bible to teach vital truths.*

It is a rather dependable rule that the Bible student who expects much from the Bible will see much; and one who dabbles in its pages for some mediocre lessons will find no more than that. The Bible is a unique book because of the *crucial* profitable doctrines which it teaches (cf. II Tim. 3:16). The most important of these concern

    a. who God is
    b. what man is
    c. what God does for man

What subjects are more vital and contemporary than these? In fact, it was to discuss these subjects that the Bible was written in the first place. Whenever you study a passage in the Bible, observe what it says about

God (Father, Son, Holy Spirit), or about man, or about God's ways with man. It is not difficult to make some personal applications based on such truths. For example, observe those truths in the following verses chosen here at random: "In that day the Lord of hosts shall be a crown of glory and a diadem of beauty to the remnant of His people" (Isa. 28:5); and "The judgment of God is according to truth against them which commit such things" (Rom. 2:2).

The Bible is also profitable for reproof, bringing conviction of sin; and for correction, showing the right way to walk. And it is profitable for instruction in righteousness, affording inspiration, challenge, example, and motivation. For *inspiration,* no passage excels Psalm 23. No *challenge* could be more timely than that of Joshua's: "Choose you this day whom ye will serve" (Josh. 24:15). *Example* appears throughout the Bible, because the Bible speaks mainly about people. Read the context of Acts 9:27 and derive an important lesson from the short phrase, "But Barnabas took him." If we are lacking *motivation* in our life for God, we can find this in such verses as I Cor. 15:58, ". . . forasmuch as ye know that your labor is not in vain in the Lord."

2. *Observe how the Bible involves you personally.*

If you think you are living in semi-privacy or isolation, think again. Inescapably, you are related in some way to God, to Satan, and to other people, as well as to yourself. Below are listed some of the involvements of such relations:

Your Relation to God
—fellowship to enjoy
—commands to obey
—promises to claim
—prayers to echo

Your Relation to Satan
—person to resist
—devices to recognize
—sins to avoid
—armor to wear

Your Relation to Others
—in the home
—in the church
—in society
—in the world

Your Own Very Being
—past heritage
—present experience
—future hope

Try reading through a chapter in the Bible, making a note of everything it says about some of the items listed above. Two suggested chapters for such an exercise are Ps. 144 and John 11.

3. *Recognize where you are in the Bible as you apply a passage.*

It is not difficult to know how to apply a simple command like "Do all things without murmurings and disputings" (Phil. 2:14). But can spiritual lessons be derived from other types of passages, such as, "David commanded to gather together the strangers that were in the land of Israel; and he set masons to hew wrought stones to build the house of God" (I Chron. 22:2)?

A key to this step of *application* is to recognize where in the scheme of the Bible the passage is located, and what kind of writing it is. It is not possible in the short scope of this book to spell this out in detail. The suggestions given below offer some help in one's application of all parts of the Bible to contemporary living.

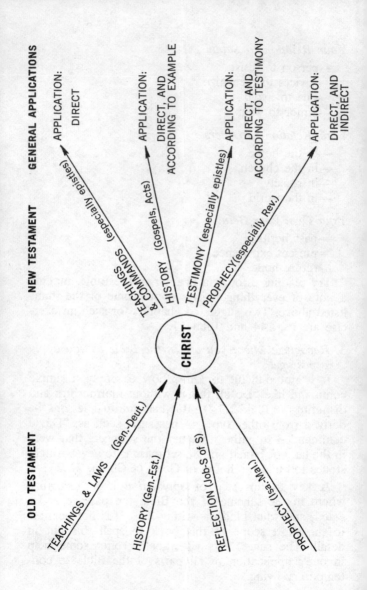

OLD TESTAMENT

TEACHINGS & LAWS (Gen.-Deut.)

HISTORY (Gen.-Est.)

REFLECTION (Job-S of S)

PROPHECY (Isa.-Mal.)

CHRIST

NEW TESTAMENT

GENERAL APPLICATIONS

TEACHINGS & COMMANDS (especially epistles)

APPLICATION: DIRECT

HISTORY (Gospels, Acts)

APPLICATION: DIRECT, AND ACCORDING TO EXAMPLE

TESTIMONY (especially epistles)

APPLICATION: DIRECT, AND ACCORDING TO TESTIMONY

PROPHECY (especially Rev.)

APPLICATION: DIRECT, AND INDIRECT

Any Bible passage which you may study has a location in the diagram on the preceeding page.

Old Testament passages are prior to Christ, thus many of these are of a Messianic nature. All New Testament passages following the Gospels were written on the basis of the death and resurrection of Christ as accomplished fact.

When you are in the Old Testament

Is the passage one of *laws?* First determine how this might relate to Christ—then involve yourself. For example, the burnt offering of Lev. 1:3 is a "male without blemish"; the offerer "shall offer it of his own voluntary will." In its present day application, Christ is the sacrifice "without blemish," and the Christian, in an act of consecration, identifies himself with Christ "of his own voluntary will."

Is the passage one of *history?* Again, the events might point forward to Christ, such as the exodus from Egypt being a type of the redemption of a sinner from the bondage of Satan. In any event, the *example* of how to approach God and live acceptably to Him appears throughout Old Testament history. Abraham's journey to the land of Canaan (Gen. 12:1-4) shows faith and obedience in action. Paul applied history like this in the following way: "all these things happened . . . for ensamples: and they are written for our admonition . . ." (I Cor. 10:11).

Is the passage one of *testimony, prayer,* or *reflection,* such as is found in the poetic and wisdom literature? It is not difficult to make applications here, for the experiences of people are universal experiences—we were all created alike, and we are all sinners in need of the same Saviour. Psalm 51, the great penitential prayer of David, is an example of Scripture that is personally applicable every day of our lives.

123

If the Scripture passage which you are reading is one of *prophecy,* you are reminded as you read that God is an omniscient Designer and sovereign Master of history. Regardless of what the prophecy is about, studying Bible prophecy should stir within your heart an increased devotion and faith in your God and Saviour. If the Old Testament prophecy has been fulfilled, such as the death of Christ foretold in Isaiah 53, apply the passage to your life in view of the event's accomplishment. If the prophecy is yet to be fulfilled, such as the Lord's coming and the Great Tribulation foretold by Daniel, respond fervently to the reminder of the urgency of the days in which you are living.

When you are in the New Testament

The New Testament is usually easier to apply than the Old Testament, mainly because we are living in the same age as its writers and original readers. The applications themselves are generally the same as for the Old Testament, since the same *kinds* of writings comprise the New Testament:

1. Teachings and commands—found especially in the epistles. Applications are usually direct, clear and timeless. For example, "Let us love one another" (I John 4:7).

2. History—mainly the Gospels and Acts. Sins to avoid and examples to follow abound here.

3. Testimony—found especially in the epistles. True Christians join in heart with the New Testament writers whenever a testimony is read, such as Paul's "I know whom I have believed, and am persuaded that he is able to keep that which I have committed unto him against that day" (II Tim. 1:12).

4. Prophecy—found throughout the New Testament, but especially in Revelation. Studying prophecy increases one's faith, inspires service in the Gospel to

lost souls, and is an incentive to righteous living. Peter said, "Seeing then that all these things shall be dissolved, what manner of persons ought ye to be in all holy conversation and godliness, looking for and hasting unto the coming of the day of God . . .?" (II Pet. 3:11-12).

The key to discovering the application of a Bible passage, especially in the Old Testament, is to derive the universal, timeless principle involved in the temporally-bound account. In studying such a biblical passage, the local temporal detail must first be identified. "Remember the sabbath day, to keep it holy" (Ex. 20:8). Here the Jewish calendar is the temporal detail; a universal principle, applicable to both Old and New Testament times, is that we should observe one designated day of the week especially as a holy day unto the Lord. Consider another example. "Achan . . . took of the accursed thing: and the anger of the Lord was kindled against the children of Israel" (Josh. 7:1). The story goes on to relate that Israel lost heart and thirty-six men were slain—all because of one man's sin. Such was the local event of that moment. A timeless universal principle to be derived from the story is that the sin of one man in a group is bound to affect the whole group adversely.

* * *

We have been discussing in this chapter some of the ways of applying the Bible to everyday life. Surely, it is not enough merely to know what the Bible *says*. Paul in his letter to Titus spoke of the need of *adorning* the doctrine of God (Titus 2:10), and throughout the letter he showed that good *deeds* were that adorning (e.g., 2:14). While James' emphasis was, "Faith without works is dead," Paul's emphasis was, "Doctrine without deeds is bare."

125

If we truly enjoy reading and studying the Bible, we will enjoy putting it to practice. The psalmist was so thrilled about the Scriptures that he exclaimed,

"O how love I thy law!
It is my meditation all the day" (119:97).

Seven lines later he supported this testimony with a word about deeds:

"I have refrained my feet from every evil way,
That I might keep thy word" (119:101)

May such practical *enjoyment* of God's Word be our daily portion!

APPENDIX

READING THROUGH THE BIBLE IN 3 YEARS

	FIRST YEAR	SECOND YEAR	THIRD YEAR
JAN.	MARK	PSALMS 42-72	I and II KINGS
FEB.	GENESIS	ROMANS & HEBREWS	PSALMS 107-150
MAR.	GENESIS	ECCLESIASTES	JEREMIAH - LAMENTATIONS
APR.	ACTS	NUMBERS	EZRA - NEHEMIAH - ESTHER
		JOB	SONG of SOLOMON
MAY	EXODUS	GALATIANS to COLOSSIANS	I and II CHRONICLES
JUNE	PSALMS 1-41	DEUTERONOMY	HOSEA to MALACHI
JUL.		I PETER to III JOHN	JAMES, JUDE, PHILEMON
AUG.	MATTHEW	PSALMS 73-106	ISAIAH
SEP.	LEVITICUS	JOHN	I TIM. - TITUS - II TIM.
OCT.	PROVERBS	JOSHUA	
		JUDGES - RUTH	
NOV.	EZEKIEL-DANIEL	CORINTHIANS-THESSALONIANS	LUKE
DEC.	REVELATION	I and II SAMUEL	

The above sequence has been arranged with topical order and variety in mind. As you begin each new book, determine the length of each daily reading, according to the time-span allotted.